M. Holmes Hartshorne

KIERKEGAARD GODLY DECEIVER

*The Nature and Meaning of
His Pseudonymous Writings*

Columbia University Press
NEW YORK

Columbia University Press
New York   Oxford
Copyright © 1990 Columbia University Press
All rights reserved

Library of Congress Cataloging-in-Publication Data

Hartshorne, M. Holmes.
Kierkegaard, godly deceiver: the nature and meaning
of his pseudonymous writings/M. Holmes Hartshorne.
p. cm.
Includes bibliographical references.
ISBN 0-231-07232-5
1. Kierkegaard, Søren, 1813-1855—Authorship. I. Title.
B4378.P74H37 1990
198'.9—dc20   90-1383
            CIP

Casebound editions of Columbia University Press books are Smyth-sewn
and printed on permanent and durable acid-free paper

Printed in the United States of America

c 10 9 8 7 6 5 4 3 2 1

KIERKEGAARD, GODLY DECEIVER

CONTENTS

M. HOLMES HARTSHORNE (1910–1988)
A PERSONAL REMINISCENCE
John S. Morris

Marion Holmes Hartshorne was one of the great teachers of Colgate University, a college with a tradition of good teaching, and with his death in 1988 we lost not only a great teacher and thinker, but a superb counsellor and friend.

Steve Hartshorne (for we all knew him as "Steve") was born in Englewood, New Jersey, on January 11, 1910. He began his undergraduate career at the Massachusetts Institute of Technology with a very strong interest in science but after two years decided that he wanted a broader education than he felt he was getting. He transferred to Williams College where he received his B.A. and M.A., the latter in the Philosophy of Mathematics. From Williams he went to Union Theological Seminary in New York, where he came under the strong influence of Paul Tillich. At Union he also met and, in 1939, married Ruth Scotford who had been a theology student at the seminary. After receiving his Th.D. from the seminary he was for a short time the minister of the Congregational Church at Wilmington, Vermont. Before arriving at Colgate University in 1946 he had taught at Olivet College in Michigan and at Doane College in Crete, Nebraska.

I first met Steve in 1954 after one of those coincidences that can profoundly change the course of a person's life. In June of that year my wife and I had come from Wales to the United States where I was to become the pastor of two small Presbyterian churches in rural upstate New York. The accidental discovery that I could enroll at Colgate for some courses in Philosophy led me to a seminar in Existentialism taught by Steve. It was the most demanding seminar I had ever experienced. Later it was Steve who encouraged me to enter the teaching profession. By another set of strange coincidences we became colleagues in the Department of Philosophy and Religion at Colgate in 1960.

To remember another person is to recall what is intensely personal. A memoir of Steve Hartshorne can only reflect one set of memories, yet those private memories embody the person we all knew. The private view reveals the public figure. The memories are still vivid: the intensity of argument, the echoing laughter, the concern with teaching, the time given to a student, the absorption over a plumbing problem. Above all, though, Steve will be remembered as a teacher and counsellor. His counselling and his preaching was as much teaching as his work in the classroom. Teaching was an expression of himself and of his own need to help others to understand that we all have to find a way to accept ourselves in a desolate world and, in that acceptance, find a way to accept others. He would throw himself wholeheartedly into an argument because philosophy was the arena within which the human situation was revealed.

Some of the clearest memories of Steve place him within the context of deep discussion with other members of the department. For at that time the Department of Philosophy and Religion at Colgate was a roving seminar.

When mid-morning Chapel ceased to be required at Colgate, a requirement that went the way of most others in the volatile sixties, there remained an appendage called "Chapel break," and this lingered as a time when there was a chance for a cup of coffee at the college center. It was a chance for the members of the staff to collect in various lounges to sip coffee and to swap items of staff gossip or entertain ideas of campus political intrigue. The members of the Philosophy and Religion Department would gather one by one in their department lounge in the basement of gaunt old East Hall. With the sipping of the coffee the conversation would usually begin with current campus gossip or the current absurdity that had come from the Administration. Inevitably some philosophical or theological issue that had come up in someone's class in our general education course in Philosophy and Religion, which we all had to teach, would energize the room, and lively, sometimes contentious, debate would follow. The Existentialist, the Wittgensteinian, the Naturalist, the Barthian would all get into the tournament of ideas. The battle would be intense but not with victory as the objective; rather, the aim was how the discussion would help in teaching the issue in our classrooms.

Each morning the coffee break became a seminar, and more often than not Steve Hartshorne was in the middle of the fray. The department lounge was, Steve often argued, our laboratory. This was the place where in the haphazard encounters of the day we could enter into the discussion that was our lifeblood as teachers and thinkers. For Steve, this discussion, conversation, and occasional intense argument made our teaching an opportunity to teach each other in the most active way possible.

Steve's engagement with the argument was, however, characteristic of his own understanding of himself as a teacher, for what captured his attention the most about the issues and items discussed was not so much their historical place in the body of a philosopher's ideas as the way in which they were a means to understand the human condition. In this he was the astute pupil of his beloved teacher, Paul Tillich. Tillich's method of correlation, set forth in *Systematic Theology* (1951), in which the contents of the Christian faith are explained through "existential questions and theological answers in mutual interdependence" (p. 68), explains much in Steve's method of argument, his method of teaching, and his style of preaching.

To read in Augustine's *Confessions:* "I had my back to the light and my face was turned towards the things which it illumined, so that my eyes, by which I saw the things which stood in the light were themselves in darkness," was to find a way of understanding the situation in which we live our intellectual lives, whatever the contextual analysis of the passage might be. It was the way in which such a passage enlightened our present intellectual condition that made Augustine's insight important and significant.

Steve's acceptance of the Tillichian claim that the questions implied in human existence emerge from the analysis of our situation led him into a study of Existentialism and into the study of Depth Psychology. The three things that were at the core of his intellectual life—teaching, counseling and preaching—were significantly affected by his studies in these areas, and one was always conscious of the use to which they were being put.

Although he has a strong intellectual grasp of the Existentialist philosophers, the deepest interest in those years during which he was teaching was in the way in which Existentialism as a philosophy gave us an understanding of the human condition. This concern led Steve almost inevitably to the deeper study of Kierkegaard. In his seminar on Existentialism, where I first came to know him as my teacher, one could almost sense the quickening of the mind in the section in which he dealt with Kierkegaard. *The Sickness Unto Death* became a central text for the course, and one could see along the way how his involvement in the work began to be important in his understanding of the world.

At this point in Steve's teaching life his work on Kierkegaard was beginning to take on a deeper fascination. In the early sixties he began to learn Danish in earnest, and after a Sabbatical year in Denmark his grasp of the subtle mind of the thinker became very clear to all who worked with him. In time the Existentialism seminar made way for a course on Kierkegaard alone, and it joined his course on Depth Psychology as one of those that serious students should on no account miss before they left the college.

Steve was always regarded as one of the finest teachers at Colgate. His courses were always very well subscribed, but his course on Depth Psychology invariably had a waiting list. In the course he was able to bring the insights of Tillich, Rollo May, Karen Horney, Jung, and Freud to the day-to-day lives of students who had only begun to wrestle with their emerging identities. He was able to do this with a level of sensitivity accompanied with a scholarly depth and perceptive understanding that few of us who engage in the give-and-take of the classroom are able to achieve. He would enter a classroom that was hushed with expectation, an expectation that would be fulfilled. No one who followed his lectures would leave without some measure of deeper understanding of the self and one's place in the network of relationships that creates our world. His course was an extraordinary exposure to the nature of the human question, and what remained in the minds of the students was the sense that here was a teacher who seemed to be able to reach to the depth of their very being, to sense the perplexities of their existence, and through the abundant readings enable them to find clues to self-understanding.

All this he did without making claims to truth and certainty. Steve never taught *about* a position; he always taught as one who had faced the deep questions of human life and for whom the questions would always remain alive and important. "Man is the question he asks about himself, before any question has been formulated" (Tillich, p. 69). Awareness of this sense of his own being led Steve always to be deeply aware of his own fragile finite nature.

At the heart of his understanding of human nature was the sense that human finitude and fallibility call into question all absolute claims to rightness. Students intensely skeptical in their sophomoric security were reminded in his baccalaureate sermon, June 1975, that there is a fundamental difference between such easygoing posturing and the radical doubt "to which a man is driven who will not evade the inner claims of truth and duty, who with absolute seriousness must wrestle with the question of his life's meaning."

Many students came to this course at first with the unstated, perhaps even unthought, hope that they would be able to engage in some easy psychoanalysis. It took only a few minutes of the first lecture before they realized that some of those expectations obviously would not be fulfilled. Those with no serious academic purpose would soon wander away never to return.

One would encounter the question of the human predicament in these intense lectures, but only if there was a willingness to place the mind deliberately at the service of the intellectual depth that the course demanded. The probity of the mind of the teacher demanded a like integrity respecting the subject matter from the student. It was difficult to trivialize either the subject matter one dealt with or the way in which the subject matter related to one's existence. The readings were exhausting as well as exhaustive; class sessions were exciting and stimulating, but they were also filled with careful thinking and vitalizing discussion. In the midst of the enthralling experience of the classroom Steve would remind every one of the temptation that every enraptured moment contained and brought us face to face with the deceptive nature of being captured by ideas themselves. In the moment when it appeared that a new freedom had been won or that one had achieved a fascinating new self-understanding, Steve made everyone think enough to think twice; ideas and language, he implied, were security blankets that could only serve to shield us from the real truth that comes with finitude and not with certainty.

He slowly peeled off the layers of certainty that we place about ourselves to hide from the truth that there is no certainty. The course put the existential question before the students, but it was done with intellectual honesty by a probing and honest mind. The teacher had himself encountered the uncertainties and fallibilities of human existence.

This same style of bringing students to encounter the truth about themselves and their situation permeated his other very popular course, "The Introduction to Religion." The essence of the course appeared in his book *The Faith to Doubt* (1963). The very basis of the course lay in his view that criticism of religion is both a "sign of sickness and health" (p. 3). Criticism reveals "the profound alienation of contemporary man from himself and his world, his sense of homelessness and meaninglessness" (ibid). It is a sign of health because the superstition of the age is unmasked.

In a sermon he preached in 1955 at the Colgate University Chapel Steve talked about the central experience of the Christian faith as being "the presence of God in those very situations where our attempts to guarantee his presence collapse. His presence is not visible to the eye that searches for security. He is not present to the man who looks for the end of danger and doubt and evil and death, who seeks to escape the burden of life."

Steve's life reflected his own search for a way of living on the edge of insecurity. Time and time again he exclaimed upon his own folly in trying to escape the burden of life. It was from this sense of his own experience that he tried to help others through his work as a counsellor. Throughout his career at Colgate he was called upon to help his students and friends, for he was a perceptive and accepting person. He was a discerning counsellor. His view of the purpose of counselling was perhaps best put by himself in an unpublished sermon on Love that he preached in 1958 at the Colgate University Chapel: "Love . . . belongs to the depth and center of life, and he who does not love is estranged from life: he is cut off from himself, from others, and from God. Love is the substance of our life as persons: it is our power to create, our power to go beyond ourselves without thereby losing ourselves—the power to give myself totally to another without destroying myself through bondage to him, and find in the relationship the fulfillment of myself as a person." He offered to many bewildered students the first helping hand; and it was his insight, integrity, and probing questioning that were paramount in his success as a counsellor.

It was this emphasis on love and these qualities of insight, integrity, and a probing questioning mind that characterized his life both as a teacher and as a colleague. It was with these that he touched so profoundly my own professional life and the lives of so many others. His intellectual probing prompted unanswerable challenges to the certainties that sustain daily life. He did not issue those challenges to make someone feel uncomfortable; and one knew that they were elicited by a man whose personal support encouraged rather than denegrated each meager attempt at creating a world for oneself. That personal support came from experiences that were just like our own.

He and I often joked—two introverts that we were, understanding each other perfectly well—about how we put our world together by an unvarying routine as we got up in the morning. To us, morning cereal was more than food; it was a rite of passage from darkness to light. Having put his world together, Steve went through each day with an unpretentious sense of its fragility. That is why he fought hard to keep his world together and why he was always aware of the power of despair and anxiety.

Through those anxieties he taught us that the truth about the world did not lie in the perfection of the created artifact of a world but in the very fragility of what we had pieced together. He forced us to the edge of our certainties and made us face the power that was present despite the brokenness of the world about us.

There was no sentimentality in his world. Sentimentality could only be an artificial covering over of the doubt, risk, and anxiety in life. As a consequence his reaching out to us in fellowship was filled with the recognition of our common human limits. In reaching out to others he disclosed an openness filled with the hope that in this there was reciprocation.

It was in this reaching out and the reciprocal act of acceptance that life was made meaningful for him and touched all his daily activities. The integrity of his teaching arose from this way of approaching life. His teaching was a lived thought and did not arise from abstract categories unrelated to life but flowed from his own sense of the fragility of life. Life itself, its meaning and its lived purpose, was revealed for him in its loneliness, frustration, forsakenness, and finitude. In this sense of his life he discovered his own experience of the meaning of the central symbol of his faith, the Cross. His teaching centered upon the meaning given to human existence through our encounter with the limits of existence when we face life's reality and are no longer able to avoid the encounter with truth, when we encounter the reality of God.

In his dying he continued to teach us. In his painful encounter with his approaching death he recognized its power as one that was overcome by his acceptance of its reality, a reality in which God's presence is made known. "It is an awesome thing," he said in his last sermon at Colgate, "to encounter God and stand defenseless against His command that we worship Him alone and that we love, not just tolerate, our neighbor." In his last sacrament of suffering and death he taught us something of the awesome moment of that defenseless acceptance of a deeper love than ours. His living embrace of family and friends in the inevitability of the moment of death made that despairing moment a sacrament in which we all participated.

He concluded the last sermon he was to preach before his death with an understanding of his own and our predicament that was characteristic of him: "As to Ezekiel of old [God] says to us in our hurt and loneliness, 'Son of man, stand upon your feet and I will speak to you.' Hear that word, and you will find the peace that God has given you. You will find the one who long since has sought you and found you. Amen." It was a genuine commentary upon his own life.

Union College
Office of the President
Schenectady, New York

PREFACE

Our western history has given us two great ironists: Socrates and Kierkegaard. They are, of course, related as teacher and pupil. Kierkegaard was profoundly influenced by Socrates, writing his master's thesis (the equivalent of the modern Ph.D. dissertation) on the concept of irony with special reference to Socrates, and, in his pseudonymous works, he gave expression to the irony he had met in Socrates.

Irony was the heart of Socrates' pedagogy: to feign ignorance in order to invite presumption, and then by questioning to disclose to the one who thought he knew, that he did not know, and thus to lead him into a nearer relation to the truth.

In a similar way, Kierkegaard employed irony to deceive the reader into the truth. With him, however, the deception was far more elaborate, far more subtle. His pseudonymous books were a grand deception, intended to engage, at the outset, the reader's interest and acceptance and then, gradually, to lead him to discover that the point of view which he had accepted uncritically (and which, to some degree, had characterized his life to that point) was totally untenable, perhaps even shockingly repugnant. In this way, the reader might glimpse the truth that was calling his previous point of view into question.

While it has been commonly recognized that Kierkegaard is an ironist, the consequences of this for the interpretation of his writings are widely overlooked. (The appendix gives a sampling of the great variety of Kierkegaard interpretation.) As Kierkegaard himself insisted, the perspective and views of his pseudonyms cannot be ascribed to him. "In the pseudonymous works there is not a single word which is mine."[1] Kierkegaard's disclaimer is generally taken to be a kind of poetic exaggeration, not—as he intended— the literal truth. Almost without exception, the interpreters of Kierkegaard have, in varying degrees, yielded to the temptation to find his beliefs in the assertions of his pseudonyms. For example, his parody of the philosophy of religion (or philosophical theology)—I have in mind, of course, *Philosophical Fragments* and the *Concluding Unscientific Postscript*, both written by that dilettante, Johannes Climacus—is taken by many to be a statement of Kierkgaard's own position. *Fear and Trembling* is presumed to be an exposition of his view of faith. To ignore Kierkegaard's warning against ascribing the perspectives and views of the pseudonyms to him leads inevitably to a misinterpretation of his writings. One will not discover Kierkegaard's own beliefs in his pseudonymous works.

This is the thesis to be developed in this volume. It is but an exposition of Kierkegaard's own statement[2] of the significance of his pseudonymous authorship. In the following pages, we shall examine some of the pseudonymous works, with a view to showing both their ironic character and the serious purpose that informed the deception which Kierkegaard so carefully carried out. We shall also consider two of his religious works in order to contrast his own position with the views of the pseudonyms. Kierkegaard was utterly serious in his contention that he was a religious writer in the service of Christianity. He was also a highly subtle one and, with the great majority of his readers then and now, he doubtless failed in his purpose because of it. Once, however, the radically ironic character of his pseudonymous writings is clearly recognized, together with the overall objective that informs them, the power and purpose of Kierkegaard's work become clear—and his genius as well. Toward the realization of this end these few pages are written.

The sources for the excerpts from Kierkegaard which I have quoted are translations that are in common use. Where it has seemed to me that the Danish has required a change in the English text, I have altered the translation or, in many cases, substituted my own. References to Kierkegaard's papers and journals are to the

Danish edition, *Søren Kierkegaards Papirer*, København, 1968; the translations from the journals are for the most part mine.

This book would not have seen the light of day without the help of many persons. I can mention only a few. I am deeply indebted to former colleagues at Krabbesholm Højskole, especially its principal, Kristian Schultz Peterson, who have contributed inestimably to my understanding and appreciation of Denmark and its language; to Steven Englund, former student and loyal friend, for his encouragement, criticism, and professional assistance; and to my wife, Ruth, without whose gentle prodding I would not have bought the computer and written this or any other book. I am grateful to them all.

M.H.H.
Hamilton, New York
July 1986

I would like to take this opportunity to express my appreciation to some of the many people who have helped in the publication of this book. First and foremost, I would like to thank my good friend John S. Morris, President of Union College, for his excellent and very thoughtful foreword to the book and its author. Two former students have been of particular help, Alan Greenberg, with his very knowledgeable indexing, and Tom O'Brien, with his superb editing. Kate Wittenberg and Louise Waller of Columbia University Press have been diligent, patient, and helpful in the publication of this book.

And most important, I would like to add my own personal thanks to Steven Englund for all his help and particularly for his skill and perseverance in shepherding the book, and me, through the publication process.

Ruth Scotford Hartshorne
Hamilton, New York

KIERKEGAARD, GODLY DECEIVER

CHAPTER ONE

One of the most distinctive features of Kierkegaard's literary work is the large number of his books which were written pseudonymously. Ostensibly, these books are not by Kierkegaard at all; their authorship is ascribed to such characters as Johannes de silentio or Judge William or Johannes Climacus—to name just a few. In some cases Kierkegaard's name appears as the publisher. What was the point of this extensive pseudonymous authorship and what is its significance for an understanding of his work? There is no doubt that Kierkegaard set pen to paper and that these books were among the resulting production. In a concluding note, that was bound unpaged at the end of the *Concluding Unscientific Postscript*, he explicitly declares that he is *not* their author. "In the pseudonymous works," he writes, "there is not a single word that is mine. . . . I am just as far from being Johannes de silentio in *Fear and Trembling* as I am from being the knight of faith he depicts." Kierkegaard took his distance from the pseudonyms with radical seriousness. Not all of his interpreters have been as scrupulous.

Some light may be shed upon this problem by a brief consideration of his life's story. Kierkegaard was unquestionably a brilliant thinker and a master of the Danish language. Born in that market town, Copenhagen, in the year 1813, when his father was almost fifty years of age, Søren had a curious childhood, if childhood it could be called. The elder Kierkegaard, though peasant-born, had become by the time of Søren's birth a wealthy merchant with good connections. The family lived in a substantial house on Nytorv. Michael Kierkegaard was a very religious man, also an extremely melancholic one, both of which characteristics he passed on to his youngest son. Søren was a strange person—old before he was even a youth, possessed of a brilliant, reflective, imaginative mind that inhabited a weak, spindly body. From his childhood he was witty, entertaining, ironic, serious, melancholic, concealing his perpetual unhappiness beneath a lighthearted exterior. The portrait of "The Unhappiest Man" in the essay by that title in *Either/ Or* describes also the young Søren: "He cannot become old, because he has never been young; in a way he cannot die, because he has not lived; in a way he cannot live, because he is already dead."[1]

Throughout his life Kierkegaard had few friends, although he could move, when he chose, in the highest social circles. There were many in Copenhagen who knew him, including the king. He was fond of taking walks in the streets of the city and, on these occasions, he enjoyed talking to children and the common folk. But his was essentially a solitary existence, his loneliness relieved only by his sense of the presence of God—and this especially in his later years.

During his early years as a university student Kierkegaard did not take his studies seriously, preferring elegant clothes, expensive food, taverns, and the theater, through all of which he tried to escape his childhood's dark days. It was all in vain. He was too deeply stamped with the penitential religious attitude of his youth and burdened as well with his melancholy. At the age of twenty-three he wrote in his journal, "I have just come from a gathering where I was the life of the party; witty remarks streamed from my mouth, everyone laughed, admired me——but I left (that dash ought to be as long as the earth's radius)——and wanted to shoot myself."[2]

The death of his father in 1838 (Søren was then twenty-five) shook him profoundly, and he felt himself obligated to fulfill his father's wish that he study for the ministry. Within two years—an unusually short time—he had completed his theological studies.

At this point there occurred an event of even more traumatic and enduring effect: he became engaged. Regine Olsen was only sixteen; he was twenty-seven. As the daughter of a minor but well-placed official, she belonged to one of the higher social ranks. But no sooner had Kierkegaard received her "yes" and her father's consent than he became convinced that he could not marry her; his deep melancholy would poison their marriage. He decided that the engagement had to be broken. He would not, however, compromise Regine, whom he loved. To protect her against the disgrace, which at that time would fall upon a young woman whose engagement was broken by the man, he pretended that he had never taken the engagement seriously, that he was simply a cad who had deceived her. He persuasively played the part of a playboy whose word could not be trusted, and by this clever and painful ruse (painful for both of them, for Regine was not deceived), he succeeded in his intention. Thirteen months later, Regine broke the engagement.

It was certainly a curious relationship, and both he and Regine suffered in it. Eight years later Kierkegaard wrote in his journal, "Suppose I had married her. Let's make that assumption. Then what? In the course of half a year, in less time, she would have been torn apart. There is . . . something ghostly about me, something the result of which is that no one can put up with me who has to see me day after day and thus have a real relation with me. . . . I had been engaged to her for a year and yet she didn't really know me. . . . I was too melancholy for her."[3] Marriage was simply an impossibility for them, the engagement had to be broken, and Kierkegaard fled, miserable, to Berlin. Professor Josiah Thompson has remarked that "his flight from Regine was nothing less than an especially poignant expression of his lifelong flight from the world."[4]

Kierkegaard did not, however, remain long in Germany. He soon returned to Copenhagen and began to write as one possessed. His major pseudonymous works, such as *Either/Or, Fear and Trembling*, and *Repetition*, among others, were written and published in the next few years, accompanied by a number of religious works, so-called "edifying discourses." Regine had become his muse.

In 1846 Kierkegaard was made an object of ridicule in a contemporary satirical journal, *Corsair*, edited by the young Meir Goldsmidt, who was to become one of Denmark's outstanding novelists. The incident was quite trivial and Kierkegaard had, in fact, been given praise in the piece; but he misunderstood the matter and was provoked into launching a compulsively bitter attack against the journal. A satirical exchange ensued that left Kierkegaard licking his wounds and feeling very much the martyr. Although the episode did constitute for him a temptation to martyrdom, he was too honest to yield to it. He was no hero; he knew that his existence was "a poet existence," standing always outside of what he wrote, but now he would be Christianity's poet.

> I am essentially a poet . . . In this respect I only have to humble myself beneath one thing: the fact that I have not the strength myself *to be* that which I understand. . . . I remain the unsuccessful lover with respect to *being* myself the ideal of a Christian, hence I became its poet. . . . As in the poet's song there echoes a sigh from his own unhappy love, so will all my enthusiastic discourse about the ideal of being a Christian echo the sigh: alas, I am not that, I am only a Christian poet and thinker.[5]

During these years he wrote his most notable Christian works, such as *Works of Love, Training in Christianity,* and *The Sickness unto Death.* But these years witnessed also a gradual retreat into himself as well as a renunciation of the world and of his role as a writer. For example, in 1853 he wrote in his journal: "I am becoming more and more exhausted. To produce appears to me to be almost folly. To starve, on the other hand, [appears to me] to be Christian."[6] And again, "The suffering that is characteristic of Christianity is to suffer from men. That is consonant with this: that according to Christianity to love God is to hate the world."[7] And further, "To love God is then impossible without hating people."[8] His father's melancholic religiosity had at length revealed its full power. He gave up writing, even in his journal. It appeared that his work was at an end.

Suddenly, however, Kierkegaard was off on a crusade. It occurred shortly after the death of Bishop Mynster in 1854. Mynster, who had been Zealand's[9] bishop and primate of the Danish Lutheran Church, had also been Michael Kierkegaard's pastor and spiritual adviser. He was a man of considerable worldliness as well as nobility of spirit, a combination not unusual among the top clergy of the Danish state church at that time. This distinguished man had often been in the merchant's home as far back as Søren could remember, and Søren had transferred his deep respect for his father to Mynster. This respect was, however, mixed with a considerable degree of disapproval of Mynster's worldliness. At Mynster's funeral, Professor Martensen, who had hopes of being Mynster's successor, described the deceased as "a witness to the truth." Kierkegaard, who felt that the worldly trappings which the bishop had enjoyed could not be reconciled with the poverty that Jesus had enjoined his disciples to practice, was outraged. When some weeks later Martensen received his appointment as bishop, Kierkegaard decided to speak out, launching his scathing attack on Christendom with a series of articles in the daily "Faedrelandet" [The Fatherland]. His articles provoked considerable notice and indignation. Later he published his own little sheet, which he called "The Instant" [Øjeblikket], and continued his strong attack on the church and its corruption (as he believed) of true Christianity.

This short but intense undertaking freed Kierkegaard from his characteristic reflective stance and gave him, probably for the first time in his life, an experience of immediacy, of spontaneity. Exhausted by this final effort, his considerable private fortune virtually gone (he was a lavish spender always), he died in Frederiks Hospital in November 1855 at the age of forty-two.

This brief sketch of Kierkegaard's life will hardly suffice to indicate what a strange man he was.[10] Many scholars have sought to explain his peculiarities as well as his genius by drawing on his relationship with his father, or on his unhappy school days, when he defended himself with merciless tongue against hazing and ridicule, or by his strange relationship with Regine Olsen, whom he could not keep, yet in imagination could not let go of. This kind of inquiry is inevitable, legitimate, and interesting, provided only that it does not compromise the integrity of Kierkegaard's thought. He had something to say, and it is worth hearing. To discover this, one must first be clear about the nature and meaning of the pseudonymous authorship,[11] which constituted in the main his aesthetical production.

An understanding of Kierkegaard's pseudonymous authorship requires that one should be clear about two things. The first is his use of the term *aesthetic (aesthetics, the aesthetical)*. In Kierkegaard's usage, the term "aesthetics" has a meaning rather different from its common meaning in English. This is clearer in the Danish than in translation. Gyldendal's *Dictionary of the Danish Language* [Ordbog over det Danske Sprog], the standard for the Danish language, includes, in addition to definitions with which we are familiar in English, the following: "pertaining to a person's philosophy of life, as this is determined by the fact that the person exclusively or to a great extent values life's various relationships on the basis of their possibility of evoking a strong feeling of pleasure, enjoyment, and the like." In Kierkegaard's usage, the aesthetical person (or aesthete) lives by pursuing what gives him pleasure, what interests him, what relieves him of boredom, what appears to be expedient—in a word, he lives like any of our contemporaries for whom happiness, freedom from boredom and fun are decisive.

The second thing about which one should be clear is the pervasiveness of irony in Kierkegaard's pseudonymous writings. The title of his master's thesis was *The Concept of Irony with constant reference to Socrates.* Had he not been a Christian, Kierkegaard would, I am persuaded, have found divinity in that Greek philosopher, whose use of irony evoked his highest admiration. This reflects, no doubt, the deeply ironic character of Kierkegaard himself, a characteristic, incidentally, that runs deep in the Danish character.[12] As an ironist Kierkegaard was certainly no cultural anomaly; but it must be added that he was ironic in the extreme. Here is a short passage from his thesis, in which he contrasts direct communication (in which the speaker says what he means) with the ironic:

> If I am conscious when I speak that what I say is my meaning, and that what is said is an adequate expression of my meaning, and if I assume that the person with whom I am speaking comprehends perfectly the meaning of what I have said, then I am bound by what is said. . . . If on the other hand what is said is not my meaning, or is the opposite of my meaning, then I am free both in relation to others and in relation to myself.[13]

As Thompson says, "the freedom of the ironist is to be absent from his words." Kierkegaard continues:

> The most common form of irony is when one says something seriously which is not seriously intended. The other form of irony is when one says something facetiously . . . which is intended seriously.[14]

The ironist thus seeks to deceive, as Kierkegaard did in his pseudonymous works, although the purpose of the deception can be (as it was in his case and with Socrates) to nudge the one deceived into discovering the truth. In *The Point of View* Kierkegaard writes:

> From the overall standpoint of the entire production of my work as an author, the aesthetic production is a deception, and in this lies

the deeper meaning of its "pseudonymity." Now a deception—that is of course an ugly thing. But to this I would reply: one should not let oneself be deceived by the word "deception." One can deceive a person for the sake of the truth, and one can, to recall old Socrates, deceive a person into the truth. Actually it is only in this way that one can bring a person who is under an illusion into the truth—by deceiving him.[15]

Later in the same book Kierkegaard elaborates this in relation to his own work.

> What does it mean to speak of "deceiving"? It means that one does not begin *right off* with the matter that one intends to deal with; one begins by taking the other person's delusion at face value. One begins, that is, (to continue with this writing's essential theme) not by saying, I am Christian, you are not; but this way: you are a Christian, I am no Christian.[16] Nor does one begin in this way: it is Christianity that I am preaching, while you are living simply by aesthetical considerations. No, one starts this way: let us talk about the aesthetical. The deception lies in the fact that one speaks in this way precisely in order to come to the religious.[17]

Kierkegaard did not mean that one begins with the aesthetical simply in order to end with a proclamation of Christian doctrine. One arrives at the religious precisely in the discovery of the aesthetical's true meaning: despair, as this becomes clear through the ironic presentation of it.

To illustrate Kierkegaard's use of irony in the pseudonymous authorship and the way in which he went about realizing his larger purpose, we turn to a consideration of his most lyrical book, *Fear and Trembling*, which ostensibly deals with faith. The book's author, Johannes de silentio, is an enthusiastic admirer of Abraham, whom he acknowledges to be "the father of faith." Johannes' problem is that he simply cannot understand how Abraham was able to have faith. Johannes is able to analyze faith into its component movements, but how to perform these movements is beyond him.

Johannes' reflections on the problem of faith center around the story of Abraham's sacrifice of Isaac. In the biblical story, Abraham was commanded by God to sacrifice his dearly beloved son, Isaac—the son of his very old age and heir to the promise which God had made to Abraham, that he would be the father of a great nation in whom all the families of the earth would be blessed.

7

Abraham obeys God, rides with Isaac to Mount Moriah, builds the altar, binds his son, and raises the knife. That God let him off the hook, as it were, by the providential substitution of a ram is, in Johannes' view, beside the point. In obedience to God, Abraham journeyed three days, built the sacrificial altar, bound the boy, drew the knife. The ethical expression for what Abraham would do is murder; the religious expression is that he was willing to sacrifice to God his son and his hopes, because God required it of him. But what makes murder a holy act? Johannes is overwhelmed at the thought of the profound anxiety that Abraham must have experienced. Yet, Abraham did it, confident that God would keep his promise, and that he, Abraham, would receive Isaac again.

Johannes further points out that the word that came to Abraham was a private word: no one else heard it or could have heard it. There was, therefore, no way for Abraham to justify himself. When we act ethically, we appeal to the universal moral law—in this case, you shall not kill. But, clearly, God's command to Abraham to sacrifice Isaac was no universal demand laid on all men. Moreover, it violated the moral law given by God himself. How could Abraham trust the word of God that commanded him to act, contrary to God's own law? A word, furthermore, that represented a reneging of God's promise to Abraham that he would make him the father of a great nation, a future to which Isaac's life was clearly indispensable? Was Abraham responding to God's word or to some demonic impulse in his own psyche? How profound must have been Abraham's dread! But Abraham believed.

For Abraham is the father of faith. This, Johannes never doubts. His difficulty is that the secret of Abraham's faith completely eludes him; yet, he devotes his book to an attempt to understand it. What he discovers is that Abraham has made two movements—the two movements of faith—and they are incommensurable. The first movement of faith he calls the movement of infinite resignation. Abraham willingly gives up what is most precious to him, because God requires it. More than that, Abraham gives up the very possibility of justifying himself, because he is not acting in conformity with the universal moral law but contrary to it; he is acting in obedience to a word that comes to him and to him alone. As far as Johannes is concerned, the movement of infinite resignation is one that any man worth his salt could and would make. Only persons of weak character—"softies," as he calls them—would welch on a task divinely given. Courage alone is all that such a task requires.

But faith, as it is exemplified by Abraham, entails a second movement as well, one that is opposite to the movement of infinite resignation and is made simultaneously with it. Thus Abraham can move to sacrifice Isaac, confident that God will not go back on his promise. He is certain that he will receive Isaac again. Moreover, he believes that God will not let him violate the divine law. Abraham can sacrifice Isaac in the full confidence that he will not transgress the moral law and that he will not lose Isaac but will receive him again. Sublime faith! Writes Johannes: "By faith Abraham did not give Isaac up, but by faith Abraham received Isaac."[18]

Yet, is not Abraham's intention to slay Isaac a clear violation of the divine prohibition against murder? Johannes is resourceful. In Abraham's case, he argues, there must be a teleological suspension of the ethical. The moral law is suspended for the sake of a higher *telos* or purpose, namely, that this act of faith shall be a sacrifice and not a murder. Johannes drains the cup of pathos:

> In the moment [Abraham] is ready to sacrifice Isaac the ethical expression for what he is doing is this: he hates Isaac. But if he really hates Isaac, he can rest assured that God does not require this, for Cain and Abraham are not identical. Isaac he must love with his whole soul; Since God requires Isaac, he must, if possible, love him even more, and only then can he *sacrifice* him; for it is indeed this love for Isaac that makes his act a sacrifice by its paradoxical contrast to his love for God. But the distress and the anxiety in the paradox are that he, humanly speaking, is entirely unable to make himself understandable.[19]

In sum, the movements of faith as Johannes de silentio describes them are absolutely contradictory. If Abraham is confident that in sacrificing Isaac he will get him back again, how can he then be said to be giving up anything? But if he really sacrifices Isaac, i.e., makes the movement of infinite resignation, then must not all hope of keeping his son be lost? It is just this paradoxical (or self-contradictory) leap of faith that Johannes supposes Abraham to be making: the father of faith leaps infinitely in opposite directions simultaneously—a neat trick if you can do it. (And now, perhaps, Sarah's laughter at the tent door is distinctly audible—or is it

Kierkegaard's?) Either of faith's alleged movements by itself is understandable: one can give up all because God requires it, or one can hang on to one's own, regardless of what God demands. Either alternative is clear enough. But to give up and to hold on to the same thing at one and the same time is absurd. And that is just what Johannes concludes. Abraham, he says, makes the movements of faith "by virtue of the absurd," and this, he adds in a pearl of understatement, is indeed marvelous; it is a miracle, a marvel.[20]

It may be objected that in many places (especially in the pseudonymous writings!) Kierkegaard seems to be claiming that Christian faith is faith in the absurd, because the mystery of the Incarnation—that the man, Jesus, is God; that a temporal and, hence, relative event in history is the presence of the Eternal—is *prima facia* absurd. Kierkegaard was aware that from the perspective of the unbeliever (Johannes is a case in point) the man of faith believes by virtue of the absurd. The believer's faith, however, is not in the absurd; it is in God. This point is clearly made in the following journal entry of 1850.

> The absurd is a category; it is the negative criterion of the divine, or of the relation to God. Inasmuch as the believer believes, the absurd is not the absurd—faith transforms it; but in every moment of weakness it is again for him more or less the absurd. Faith's passion is the only thing that overcomes the absurd; if it is not present, then faith is not in the strictest sense faith but a kind of knowledge. The absurd rounds off negatively the sphere of faith, which is a separate sphere. For the outsider [lit. the third party] the believer believes by virtue of the absurd; this is the way the unbeliever has to judge, for he is outside of faith's passion. Now, Johannes de silentio never claimed to be a believer, just the opposite; he declared that he was not a believer—*in order negatively to illuminate faith* [emphasis mine].[21]

Fear and Trembling is typical of the pseudonymous works, Kierkegaard's aesthetical writings. In this case the subject under discussion purports to be faith. As the analysis develops, however, it becomes increasingly clear that Johannes' notion of faith is absurd, entailing as it does the mutually contradictory movements of infinite resignation on the one hand, and the assurance of the recovery of what has been sacrificed on the other. In addition there is the preposterous (and terrifying) assumption of the teleological suspension of the ethical, which would open the door to legitimizing anything a fanatic might want to do, provided only he could persuade himself that God had spoken to him and to him alone.

What Kierkegaard is doing in *Fear and Trembling* is ironically showing the ultimate absurdity of attempting to reach faith by a mighty effort. Good Lutheran that he was, he believed that faith is a matter of grace, not of spiritual heroics. It is a gift to be accepted, not a task to be performed by spiritual gymnastics. The biblical witness is clear: God spoke to Abraham, and Abraham believed. The miracle of faith does not yield to intellectual dissection that would lay bare its human movements. The grace of God in Christ is received by faith, not achieved by spiritual movements.[22]

Fear and Trembling is ironic to the core. It pretends to be a serious analysis of faith, but it carries the reader very persuasively, very artfully and insightfully, from one absurdity to another. The irony is pervasive; for example, Johannes quotes from the New Testament and gets it wrong.[23] Johannes admires the man of faith for his awesome isolation and for his marvelous leap of faith: Abraham "performs the miraculous"; but the biblical emphasis on the enabling presence of God as the necessary condition of faith is not recognized. This last is underscored by the title, *Fear and Trembling*, which is, of course, taken from Philippians 2:12: "Work out your own salvation with fear and trembling: for God is at work in you, both to will and to work his good pleasure." In Johannes' book, it is Abraham's work that is celebrated; there is no mention of God's.

With great subtlety the reader is led down the primrose path in the hope—and here we return to Kierkegaard and his purpose in writing this book—that he will wake up and see that his common sense notions about what it is to be a Christian and to have faith, notions that he shares with all of Christendom, are absurd, if not blasphemous. What Kierkegaard is doing can best be expressed using his figure of speech: the absurdities of Johannes' thoughts about faith are put forward as good money, with the intent that the reader will accept them as such and then gradually be deceived into the truth of their illusory nature.[24]

What is to be made of this kind of pseudonymous writing? Despite Kierkegaard's clear disclaimer at the end of the *Postscript* (his assertion that not a word of the pseudonyms[25] is his), despite his own explanation in *The Point of View*, despite the omnipresent irony in his books, so well illustrated in *Fear and Trembling*, the great majority of those who write about Kierkegaard ignore his protests and attribute to him in whole or, in part, the viewpoints held by the pseudonyms. Examples are given in the Appendix.

Thus Kierkegaard, for whom faith is a miracle of grace, is presumed, on the basis of *Fear and Trembling*, to regard it as the absurd spiritual gymnastics of Johannes de silentio. His interpreters miss the irony that runs through his pseudonymous works, which may explain why so little heed is paid to Kierkegaard's own explanation of the pseudonymous authorship, as set forth by him in *The Point of View*. To be sure his accounting came toward the end—though not *at* the end—of his productive years, but it strains credibility to suppose that a man in his mid-thirties, who was still writing brilliantly, was a victim of senility. Josiah Thompson alone appears to have taken Kierkegaard at his word.[26] A careful examination of the presuppositions of the pseudonymous authors will, I am convinced, sustain Thompson's judgment.

CHAPTER TWO

The necessary starting point for any study of Kierkegaard is the recognition that he considered his entire literary activity to be a religious task. In the introduction to his posthumously published book, *The Point of View for My Work as an Author*, Kierkegaard wrote, "The content of this little book is, then: what I as a writer truly am, that I am and have been a religious author, that the whole of my activity as a writer is related to Christianity, to the problem of becoming a Christian, with a direct and indirect polemic aimed at that monstrous illusion called Christendom, or that in such a land as ours all are 'Christians'."[1] In other words, Kierkegaard wrote in order to persuade the reader, who considered himself to be a Christian, that in reality he was not one. Might he not then become one under such tutelage?

Right here we face an unyielding difficulty: one cannot be persuaded to become a Christian merely by reading something. No one becomes a believer just because another tries to demonstrate to him faith's truth; faith is not a set of beliefs whose truth can be established. That one is persuaded, for example, that God exists does not signify that one believes in God—that one trusts (has faith in) God. Faith is not a matter of knowledge or insight but of one's attitude or stance. For example, I may acknowledge that you exist, but it does not thereby follow that I put my trust in you, that I have faith in you. Belief in God means that one enters into a particular relationship to God in which one has absolute confidence in him; otherwise the word "God" has no religious meaning. To believe that God exists is not the same as having faith in God, as trusting God; belief in the existence of God merely indicates that one has a particular philosophical position of whose truth one is persuaded.

Kierkegaard was persuaded that his contemporaries were not Christian, in spite of the fact that they considered themselves to be entirely respectable Christians. In a passage which he titled "That Christendom is a monstrous illusion," Kierkegaard wrote:

> Everyone with some capacity for observation, who seriously considers what is called Christendom, or the condition in a so-called Christian country, must surely be assailed by profound misgivings. What does it mean that all these thousands upon thousands call themselves Christians as a matter of course? These many, many people, of whom the greater part, so far as one can judge, live their lives in quite different categories, something which one by the simplest observation can convince himself of! People who perhaps never once go to church, never think about God, never utter His name except when they swear! People upon whom it has never dawned that they might have any obligation to God, people who either regard it as a maximum to be guiltless of transgressing the criminal law, or do not count even this quite necessary! Yet all these people, even those who assert that there is no God, are all of them Christians, call themselves Christians, are recognized as Christians by the State, are buried as Christians by the Church, are certified as Christians for eternity! That there must here be a monstrous confusion, a terrible illusion, is beyond any doubt.[2]

A large part of Kierkegaard's work as an author was aimed at shocking and offending these proper and respectable Christians in order that they might take notice of what they really were and what Christian faith really is. He called them "Philistines" [*spidsborgers*]. The essential characteristic of the Philistine is that his life is an unconscious reflection of society's values and prejudices, i.e., of everything which his contemporaries take for granted, without his giving a single thought to the basis of these beliefs. The Philistine lives in accordance with the generally accepted customs and ideas of his time, contentedly occupied with his business and his family, his success and his happiness, as he uncritically follows society's fixed patterns. He himself, of course, believes that he is living an independent life that reflects his own decisions and choices. Indeed, he *appears* to choose between different options and to direct his life in accordance with his own interests, but in reality these choices only illustrate the social and historical forces that determine how and what he chooses. In his book, *Kierkegaards Univers*, Professor Johannes Sløk comments: "A Philistine lives out his life in the illusion that he himself has freely made the decisions which in fact anonymous forces have made for him."[3] The Philistine has no inkling of what really rules his life.

Kierkegaard's purpose as an author was to awaken these Philistines to an understanding of their spiritual condition. He was well aware of the difficulty of such an enterprise, especially of any attempt to persuade them to become Christians.

> To compel a person to accept an idea, a conviction, a belief, is something that in all eternity it is impossible for me to do, but one thing I can do . . . I can compel him to take notice.
>
> That this is a good work cannot be doubted, but it must not be forgotten that it is also a gamble. By compelling a man to take notice I also compel him to judge. Now he will judge. But what he decides is not in my power to determine. Perhaps he will decide the very opposite of what I wish. Moreover, the fact that he was compelled to judge may have embittered him, furiously embittered him, against the cause and against me. And perhaps I am the victim of my own gamble.[4]

To compel the Philistine to take notice, Kierkegaard had to make him conscious of his unconscious presuppositions, of his complete dependence upon his society's values and biases. How can such an illusion be dispelled? In Kierkegaard's view, it cannot be dispelled directly. "If the belief that everyone is a Christian is an illusion and if something is to be done about it, it must be done indirectly, not by one who vociferously proclaims himself to be an exemplary Christian but by one who, better advised, declares that he is not a Christian at all."[5] Consistent with this appraisal of human nature and hopeful of compelling some of his contemporaries to take notice, Kierkegaard began to publish a series of books, written pseudonymously, that do not deal with Christian themes but with aesthetics. He believed that to win a hearing, one must start where these so-called Christians actually are[6] and address them in the categories in which they actually live their lives, and then by irony let them, if they can or will, discover the true nature of that mode of existing. Hence, his aesthetical works.[7]

Accordingly, Kierkegaard began his work as a religious author by addressing the Philistine where he actually is: concerned with his interests and pleasures, intent upon maximizing his happiness, yet unconscious of the fact that he is not the Christian he thinks he is. Writes Kierkegaard: "The religious writer must first take care to achieve a rapport with his reader. That is, he must begin with aesthetical production."[8] Kierkegaard's aesthetical books were written in such a way that the Philistine reader might be led to confront the ultimate significance of his way of life. That is, that he might be compelled to take notice—of his own presuppositions. When the Philistine discovers that his values and decisions and his life's purpose are determined not by his choice but by the relative and accidental character of the prevailing patterns of society, he becomes disillusioned. Everything tends to become for him a matter of indifference, because no choice, no decision is finally his; it only appears to be and so is empty of self and of meaning. Because his values and duties have no absolute status in reality, not even in the reality of his own nature, they are threatened with meaninglessness. Nothing any longer can be taken seriously. "In the very moment in which the Philistine discovers that he is a Philistine, and what that means, he is immediately changed to something else. He becomes an aesthete."[9] Now he knows that choice is arbitrary. As a Philistine, innocent of any insight into his true status, he had never made any decisions; he only believed that he had. Now he knows that his choosing is and always has been empty, that it always will be empty, because the alternatives are equally without intrinsic meaning: they are the accidental dictates of the society into which he happens to have been born. Everything he does or contemplates doing becomes a matter of indifference to him. Listen to "A," the aesthete, in Kierkegaard's book, *Either/Or*:

> I don't care about anything.* I don't care about riding, it is too energetic an activity; I don't care about walking, it is too strenuous. I don't care to lie down, for either I should remain lying, and I don't care for that, or I should get up again, and I don't care for that either. *Summa summarum*: I don't care about anything. (*Perhaps more idiomatically rendered, "I don't give a damn about anything")[10]

For the aesthete, values have no relevance, because they have no objective status, no ontological reality. If the only basis for choosing one thing rather than another is that this is what people do, what people say is right, what people proclaim as duty, then values lack foundation; they are no more than the accidental characteristics of the particular society into which one happens to have been born. The aesthete perceives the folly of being constrained by any values whatever. The only basis of choice, consequently, is interest and desire—the desire to maximize one's pleasure and to avoid boredom, as well as to pursue (if one happens to feel like it) that which happens to catch one's interest at the moment. One is given over to total arbitrariness.

The aesthetical is one of three fundamental attitudes toward life. In the pseudonymous works they are called "stages." The aesthete doesn't give a damn about anything, because it is ridiculous to take anything seriously, to choose between alternatives as if the final choice made any difference at all. Here is how the aesthete "A" sums it up:

> If you marry, you will regret it; if you do not marry, you will also regret it; if you marry or do not marry, you will regret both; whether you marry or do not marry you will regret both. Laugh at the world's follies, you will regret it; weep over them, you will also regret that; laugh at the world's follies or weep over them, you will regret both; whether you laugh at the world's follies or weep over them, you will regret both. Believe a woman, you will regret it, don't believe her, you will also regret that; believe a woman or don't believe her, you will regret both; whether you believe a woman or don't believe her, you will regret both. Hang yourself, you will regret it; don't hang yourself, and you will also regret that; hang yourself or don't hang yourself, you will regret both; whether you hang yourself or don't hang yourself, you will regret both. This, gentlemen, is the sum and substance of all philosophy.[11]

It is readily apparent that such an attitude toward life is characterized by arbitrariness and indifference. Consequently, wisdom consists in enjoying whatever one can in order to avoid boredom, for boredom, according to "A," is the root of all evil. He elaborates this thesis in an entertaining essay in *Either/Or* called "The Rotation Method." This quotation captures something of its flavor:

> To start from a basic principle is affirmed by people of experience to be a very reasonable procedure; I am willing to humor them, and so begin with the principle that all men are boring. Or might there be some who would be boring enough to contradict me in this . . . ?
>
> Boredom is the root of all evil. The history of this can be traced from the very beginning of the world. The gods were bored, and so they created man. Adam was bored, because he was alone, and therefore Eve was created. From that moment on boredom entered the world and increased in proportion to the increase in the population. Adam was bored alone; then Adam and Eve were bored together; then Adam and Eve and Cain and Abel were bored *en famille*; then the population of the world increased, and the peoples were bored *en masse*. To divert themselves they conceived the idea of constructing a tower high enough to reach the heavens. This idea is just as boring as the tower was high, and constitutes a terrible proof of how boredom had gained the upper hand.[12]

And so on, in a very amusing piece with quite cynical content. In the face of the world's follies and the folly that is the world, we may as well laugh as cry; and why do one rather than the other? As far as the aesthete is concerned, it makes no difference whatever, except that the one might be more interesting than the other.

In sum, the aesthete is a former Philistine, who having discovered that fact, finds that nothing in his life any longer really matters except, perhaps, to avoid being bored. Eat, drink, and be merry, for tomorrow we die!

There is, however, another way in which a person may be shaken out of his philistinism. It turns on the discovery and affirmation of duty, of obligation, of the ethical. Instead of living a life determined by society's mores, merely reflecting the patterns of culture, the ethical person acts in accordance with duty, i.e., with norms and values which he believes to be real. Unlike the Philistine, he does not make decisions that are in blind conformity to "what is done," nor are they arbitrary and groundless, as is the case with the aesthete. The ethical individual acts, as any human being ought to act, in conformity with universal moral law. Accordingly, his life has authenticity, rescued from the arbitrariness of an aesthetical or philistine existence.

From the perspective of the ethical, the aesthete, like the Philistine, is in despair.[13] He has no self, for his decisions are mere

18

appearance and without justification. For the aesthete, choices give no structure to life; they reflect only the whims that move him. If, however, one of these despairing persons were to *choose* his despair, in the sense that he were to dare to accept the fact that his life is characterized by arbitrariness and that he is therefore in despair, if he were to accept his despairing life as his own and to take responsibility for it, then he has chosen himself, and in so doing he has acted ethically. He has decided to be who he is: one who despairs. In so deciding, he has moved beyond despair. Another element now determines his life: good and evil. Either/or is not a matter of indifference. *Choice makes a difference.*

The Kierkegaardian prototype of the ethical person is Judge William, who in Vol. 2 of *Either/Or* writes long, boring letters to his young friend, "A," the aesthete of Vol. 1., endeavoring to persuade him that he should choose despair—that is, take responsibility for his despair and in so doing choose himself "in his eternal validity," to use the judge's term.

What is the meaning of this rather presumptuous-sounding phrase? When one chooses oneself in one's eternal validity, i.e., *ethically*, one chooses an existence defined by those norms that are assumed to be valid and normative for all men, without exception. One decides to live according to those eternal principles, that absolute moral law, which hold for mankind as such. For example, the law that commands an individual to love his neighbor as himself is not a law that obtains only in certain circumstances or when the individual chooses to obey it. This law is the command to be a true human being—universal man, in the judge's parlance. To love our neighbor is our duty, and we are bound by our duty, whether we want to or no, whether we find it interesting or boring. In the judge's words, the ethical man has "clothed himself in duty; for him it is the expression of his inmost nature."[14] Duty is not external to him but in him. Therefore, "he who lives ethically expresses in his life the universal, he makes himself the universal man," for "every person is the universal man."[15]

This modest claim constitutes the foundation of the judge's ethical position. It is by virtue of our absolute choices that we establish the ethical norms that bind mankind.

It is when I choose myself absolutely, that I infinitize myself absolutely, for I myself *am* the absolute, for only myself can I choose absolutely, and this absolute choice of myself is my freedom, and only as I have chosen myself absolutely have I posited an absolute distinction, that namely between good and evil."[16]

Here, one is inevitably inclined to recall the serpent's word to Eve: "God knows that when you eat of it, your eyes will be opened, and you will be like God, knowing good and evil."[17] In the judge's view, the splendor of the ethical man is this: he is the absolute, and as the absolute he can posit the distinction between good and evil. Biblically speaking, he becomes like God. He chooses for himself and for all mankind the moral law, and it is absolute. One can readily see that Sartre's indebtedness is to Judge William, not to Kierkegaard.

Neither "A" nor Judge William speak for Kierkegaard. In Kierkegaard's view, no one becomes like God, whether (like the aesthete) by rejecting every claim of conscience or (like the ethicist) by becoming the author of one's own righteousness. To "become like God" is simply to become a sinner; no individual can become universal man. Neither can an individual live without values, constrained solely by desires which in the last analysis are purely accidental and ephemeral. The ethical stage is empty presumption; the aesthetical stage is meaninglessness. Both are despair.

Judge William's two letters to "A" are lengthy, comprising the second volume of *Either/Or* and running to about three hundred pages. Their thesis, however, can be expressed quite succinctly: Choose despair! Choose the standpoint from which despair is recognized for what it is, i.e., living amorally. To choose despair is to choose the ethical standpoint; it is to posit the universal moral law that describes our essential nature. To live ethically is to live as universal man, to live as absolute, to be absolute. It scarcely need be added that the Judge would have failed to persuade "A," since any appeal to the ethical is quite without meaning for the aesthete. Where interest and desire determine one's life, obligation and duty are without significance.

Here, then, is the "either/or" posed by the two volumes. *Either* one lives amorally, with one's actions and attitudes determined solely by interest and desire, especially the desire to avoid boredom and maximize the interesting; *or* one lives ethically, expressing in one's life the universal moral law and thus choosing oneself absolutely and thereby becoming the absolute. These are the book's alternatives: desire or duty.

Alternatives they *appear* to be, but these two stages (*stadier*) actually portray two radical extremes. On the one hand, "A" celebrates a life entirely without obligation and value, so that it is a matter of complete indifference what an individual chooses or does. Here are two examples of how "A" views life:

> My view of life is utterly meaningless, as if an evil spirit had set a pair of spectacles upon my nose, of which one lens is a tremendously powerful magnifying glass, the other an equally powerful reducing glass.
>
> Of all ridiculous things it seems to be that the most ridiculous is to be a busy man of affairs, prompt to meals, and prompt to work. Hence when I see a fly settle down at a crucial moment on the nose of a business man, or see him bespattered by a carriage which passes by him in even greater haste, or a drawbridge opens before him, or a tile from the roof falls down and strikes him dead, then I laugh heartily. And who could help laughing? What do they accomplish, these hustlers? Are they not like the housewife when her house was on fire, who in her excitement saved the fire-tongs? What more do they save from the great fire of life?[18]

Judge William, on the other hand, contends that to become oneself is to become universal man, to become absolute, to become like God, "knowing good and evil." The ethical, he declares, "construes man with a view to his perfection, sees him in his true beauty."[19] Duty lies within each of us; it is not imposed from without. In doing one's duty one is being oneself—and the absolute as well. Such is the power of choice.

Such are the extreme alternatives set forth in *Either/Or.* It is difficult to escape the conclusion that human life is described by neither but actually lies somewhere between these extremes. Indeed, it would appear that every individual's life is in part characterized by these two "stages," exemplifies in varying degrees something of each. We all seek what interests us, and we try to escape being bored. We attempt to satisfy our desires and to have a good time when it is appropriate. But we also acknowledge duty. We cannot always do what we want to do; there are many things that we must do because we ought to. These obligations constitute the necessary conditions of community. One ought, for example, to speak the truth, not because some authority demands it, but rather because our common life cannot do without it. If we cannot trust one another and believe what we say to one another, community disintegrates. We are well acquainted with both the aesthetical and the ethical, for in varying (but more modest) mixture they constitute the stuff of our ordinary existence. *They can be distinguished, but they cannot be separated.* They are unavoidable elements of human existence.

Therefore, it is not true, as some contend, that Kierkegaard thought of individuals as passing through the aesthetical stage to the ethical and then on to the religious. The aesthetical (as portrayed by "A") and the ethical (as set forth by Judge William) are not, as such, human possibilities; they are abstractions *from* human existence. Juxtaposed to each other, they describe the tension in which we all live. In themselves they are simply ironic caricatures.

If for a moment we now consider, *quite hypothetically*, these two stages as though they were separable and described real modes of existence, some points of interest come to light. From the aesthetical standpoint one cannot possibly understand the ethical, cannot comprehend what the word "duty" really means. Of course, the word itself can be understood aesthetically; that is, there are people who feel themselves compelled to do what they call their duty. The aesthete, however, would say that what these benighted souls call duty is actually something which they unconsciously desire to do, perhaps because they are fearful of punishment, perhaps because they enjoy doing it, or are praised for it, or win some kind of reward for it, etc.. In short, the aesthete can always explain the ethical in aesthetical categories, but that which constitutes the ethical, namely that one ought, under all circumstances, to do one's duty solely because it is one's duty—this the aesthete cannot understand. He will, or course, use ethical words, but he will use them without ethical meaning. For example, in the first volume of *Either/Or* Johannes the Seducer, after he has deceived an innocent young girl and got her in his power, reflects in a seemingly ethical way.

> Do I love Cordelia? Yes. Sincerely? Yes. Faithfully? Yes—in an aesthetic sense, but this also means something. What good would it have done this girl to have fallen into the hands of some dunce of a faithful husband? What would have become of her? Nothing. It is said that it takes a little more than honesty to get through the world. I would say that it takes something more than honesty to love such a girl. That more I have—it is duplicity. And yet I love her faithfully.[20]

"A" uses ethical words but without ethical significance. What is decisive for his relationship with Cordelia is her psychological and sexual unfolding as a woman through his skillful employment of his seductive wiles. To him that is intensely interesting, and for that reason it constitutes faithfulness to her. He has not the slightest inkling of the ethical significance of the ethical words he uses. From the perspective of an ethicist like Judge William, he lacks the necessary presuppositions to understand them, namely the will "to choose himself in his eternal validity." In addition, "A" is unwilling to assume responsibility for his actions in obedience to the universal moral law. For the aesthete, duty is an empty concept. Therefore, anything is possible, everything is permitted, and nothing finally escapes the fate of being boring. In the last analysis, his response to any situation is "I couldn't care less." The only "good" is to be free from boredom as long as possible and to enjoy as much as possible the accidental interests and pleasures that one may find oneself claimed by. What shall I do with my life? Enjoy it—if you can.

Just as the aesthete can both understand and not understand the ethical person, so the ethicist has a similar problem with the aesthetical man. Judge William recognizes that "A" has refused to choose himself in his eternal validity and, for that reason, cannot act ethically. But the judge is unable to believe that "A" can, at bottom, be utterly amoral. Referring to the passage quoted on page 17, "If you marry, you will regret it, if you do not marry, you will also regret it . . . ," the judge writes,

> In case this really were your serious meaning, there would be nothing one could do with you; one would have to take you as you are and deplore the fact that melancholy [literally, heavy-mindedness] or light-mindedness had enfeebled your spirit.[21]

But, Judge William is not willing to concede that the kind of attitude "A" gives voice to is possible, because he cannot conceive of a totally amoral person. Imagine, he writes to "A," a young man, wholesome, pure, intellectually gifted, rich in hope who, with confidence, turned to you for wise counsel. Would you dismiss him by saying to him that what he does is a matter of indifference? No, says the judge, you would not. His noble qualities would make you serious. "Your good nature, your sympathy, would be set in motion; in that spirit you would talk to him. You would fortify his soul, confirm him in the confidence he had in the world, you would assure him that there is a power in a man which is able to defy the whole world, and you would insist that he take to heart the importance of employing his time well. All this you can do, and when you will, you can do it handsomely."[22] In short, so far as the judge is concerned, "A" could not but act ethically toward the young man.

But, this is precisely what "A" would *not* do. He would, perhaps, do some or all of the things that the judge has enumerated, but he would do them out of an aesthetical interest in the young man. In so doing, he would be showing him the very kind of love that Johannes the Seducer showed Cordelia; he would not be acting ethically. The judge, however, is so sure of his viewpoint that he writes, "I know very well that the polemical side you turn towards the world is not your true nature."[23]

Neither "A" nor Judge William can understand each other, because Kierkegaard has created two extreme positions that lack an essential common element, namely real existence, in which the aesthetical and the ethical are simultaneously present. In our common life, these two are manifest most obviously, in the tension between what I want and what I ought. Kierkegaard's purpose was to shock his fellow Copenhageners, Philistines all, into an awareness of their spiritual condition by deceiving them into discovering for themselves the ultimate implications of their aesthetical inclinations and their moral complacency. Both of the standpoints set forth in *Either/Or* are unreal. Kierkegaard regarded the entire book as an aesthetical production. The actual alternatives posed by and in our human existence are not the aesthetical and the ethical. Rather, they are the alternatives of sin and faith, as he makes clear in *Sickness unto Death*. Moreover, these two pairs of alternatives are not parallel. The ethical has, finally, no firmer foundation than has the aesthetical; both are constructs of consciousness, that float off into the imaginary and are incapable of supporting existence.

Thus, the Philistines of Kierkegaard's day, who had an ethical concern that gave them the comfortable illusion of self-righteousness, were no further along the road of life than those whose existence was characterized by the pursuit of pleasure and profit. In his view, the city was full of both types. The dismaying truth was that these good Copenhageners had slight, if any, awareness of their spiritual condition. In spite of the fact that they imagined they were Christians, they lived without the least understanding of what it would mean to be a Christian or to live as a Christian. Here is Kierkegaard's ironic description of such a deluded existence.

> It is exceedingly comic that a person, stirred to tears, so that not only sweat but tears pour down his face, can sit and read or hear an exposition on self-denial, on the nobility of sacrificing his life for the truth—and then in the next moment, *ein, zwei, drei, vupti,* almost with tears still in his eyes, be in full swing, in the sweat of his brow and to the best of his modest ability, helping untruth to be victorious. It is exceedingly comic that a speaker, with sincere voice and gestures, deeply stirred and deeply stirring, can movingly depict the truth, can boldly face all the powers of evil and of hell, with cool self-assurance in his bearing, a dauntlessness in his air, and an appropriateness of movement worthy of admiration—it is exceedingly comic that almost in the same moment . . . he can timidly and cravenly cut and run away from the slightest inconvenience. . . . When I see someone who declares that he has completely understood how Christ went about in the form of a lowly servant, poor, despised, mocked, and, as Scripture tells us, spat upon—when I see the same person carefully make his way to the place where in worldly sagacity it is good to be, set himself up as securely as possible, when I see him then so anxiously, as if his life depended upon it, avoiding every gust of unfavorable wind from right or left, see him so blissful, so extremely blissful, so slap-happy, yes to make it complete, so slap-happy that he even thanks God for—for being whole-heartedly honored and esteemed by all, by everyone—then I have often said privately to myself: "Socrates, Socrates, Socrates, can it be possible that this man has understood what he says he has understood"[24]

No, it is quite clear that this person has not understood. His lack of understanding is due to this alone: as a Philistine, he lacks reflection. He is totally without knowledge of himself and of his superficial relationship to his values and to his self-delusion. In consequence, his relation to God, as well as God's claim upon his life, concern him not at all. Of course he does not realize this. He is a churchgoer, and he thinks that it is very important to listen to God's word—provided that he is not engaged in some business deal or other pressing activity. The only words he actually hears are those of other people. He is a typical Philistine: religious, moralistic, busy, convivial—and empty.

It may well be asked whether it is really possible for any person to deceive himself in such a straightforward manner. Kierkegaard believed that it was indeed possible and that this spiritual condition holds for the vast majority. Bluntly stated, we are all Philistines—unless (and of this Kierkegaard was very unsure, if not downright doubtful) here and there, now and then, there may be a Christian among us. The Philistine lacks the existential presuppositions for true self-knowledge; he lacks faith. He can, and doubtless will, busy himself with all kinds of "good works," attend religious services and have his children baptized and confirmed, but he is a victim of "that monstrous illusion" that is Christendom.

> The philistine/bourgeois mentality lacks every determinant of spirit and ends up in the realm of the probable, within which the possible[25] finds its insignificant place; it lacks thus any possibility of taking notice of God. Bereft of imagination, as the Philistine always is, whether alehouse keeper or prime minister, he lives in a certain trivial province of experience as to how things go, what is possible, what usually happens. In this way the Philistine has lost himself and God.[26]

Is there any escape from Philistinism? At first glance, it would appear that Kierkegaard proposes two ways out. If a person becomes conscious of his philistine condition, he immediately becomes an aesthete and can live henceforth in total indifference to all spiritual concerns, simply seeking to fulfill any desire that may happen to claim him or avoiding in any way possible the boredom that always threatens. That is apparently one way out. The other is an equally contingent possibility. A person may choose himself in his eternal validity, create the distinction between good and evil, and live secure in his own righteousness.

But Kierkegaard's description of these "escape routes" is ironic in the extreme. He recognized that we human beings are inescapably inclined to chase after pleasure and that at the same time we now and again listen to the voice of duty. The extreme ways out of philistinism that appear to be the thesis of *Either/Or* are not really existential possibilities at all. *They are extremes that can be thought, but they cannot be lived.* A modicum of reflection may cause the Philistine to take notice of his aestheticism, to realize that it is the pursuit of pleasure and the abhorrence of boredom that motivate much of his life, that these are values that he embraces. Reflection may thus cause him to recognize that values and duties do concern him, and they can tempt him to make absolute judgments, whose moral validity he does not doubt. Reflection will not take him out of existence, but it can underscore, even exacerbate, the contradiction in which he lives.

For Kierkegaard, there is only one escape from a philistine existence, only one true salvation. It is to become a Christian. But that happens only by the grace of God in Jesus Christ. It is not something we do, not a higher rung on the ladder of spiritual achievment, not a higher stage of existence. All Kierkegaard could do as a writer was to make his readers take notice. By reading, for example, *Either/Or*, the Philistine reader might perhaps discover three things. First, that he is a Philistine; second that the cultivation and increase of the aesthetical elements in life only lead to cynicism and deeper despair; third, that moral self-righteousness, based on the illusion of being the absolute, leads not to moral integrity but to overweening pride coupled with banality. Thus would Kierkegaard try to nudge the Philistine reader to—to become a Christian? No, that he could not do. One does not become a Christian by reading a book, though one may perhaps take notice. One becomes a Christian only by the grace of God in Christ. Luther's confession lives on in Kierkegaard: salvation is by divine grace through faith in Jesus Christ.

CHAPTER THREE

The preceding chapters disclose quite clearly that three factors exercised a decisive influence upon Kierkegaard and upon his writing: irony, melancholy, and Christianity. The most enduring and also the most powerful was Christianity. Kierkegaard understood his task as an author to be a Christian vocation; it was one which had two very distinct and very different components. The pseudonymous writings were written in the hope that some who regarded themselves as Christians, but were not, might be compelled to take notice. His reflective mind enabled Kierkegaard to lay bare with surgical skill the distortions and pretensions of Danish Christendom. In this endeavor his weapon was irony.

In addition to the pseudonymous writings Kierkegaard also wrote Christian works, such as *Works of Love,* in which he set forth, without irony, his understanding of the Gospel in its purity.

His melancholy, which at times could sound like cynicism, characterized much of the aesthetical production, most obviously in the first volume of *Either/Or.* In a very real sense it underlay all of the early aesthetical works, because it was the reason for his break with Regine Olsen, and that event, in turn, was the immediate occasion of his writing *Either/Or, Fear and Trembling,* and *Repetition.*

In this chapter we consider two of his more philosophical pseudonymous writings, which deal with Christian themes. They too are laced with his characteristic irony, though the irony is extremely subtle—so much so that many take them to be an exposition of Kierkegaard's theological position. Such a conclusion is very far from being the case.

Concluding Unscientific Postscript, translated by David F. Swenson and Walter Lowrie, was the first major work of Kierkegaard to be published in English. This large volume, which in the English translation runs to some five hundred and fifty pages, is by Johannes Climacus and is a promised postscript to his slim little volume entitled *Philosophical Fragments.*[1] Together they constitute an impressive philosophical production. Christianity is not mentioned in *Fragments,* although it is obviously in the writer's mind. The *Postscript,* on the other hand, appears to be an attempt to set forth a Christian position.

In any consideration of these books, one must first take note of their author. They are written by Johannes Climacus, not by Kierkegaard. Moreover, it is at the end of the *Postscript* that one finds Kierkegaard's emphatic disclaimer, that not a word of the pseudonyms is his, that he is not the author of their books. It can be argued, of course, that since in one sense—for many it is the most important sense—Kierkegaard *is* their author, he could not finally escape being their creator, even if he wanted to distance himself from these books' contents. The presumed conclusion from this line of reasoning is that the pseudonyms do express Kierkegaard's own views, though perhaps somewhat veiled. This dispute is best clarified, if not decided, by looking at the books themselves.

Philosophical Fragments begins with the question, "How far does the Truth admit of being learned?" It straightway becomes apparent that the Truth here at issue is the Truth by which one can live an authentic life. This question, Johannes points out, is the Socratic one, and entails essentially the problem posed in the dialogue, *Meno.*

> One cannot possibly seek for what he knows, and it is equally impossible for him to seek for what he does not know; for what he knows, he cannot seek, since he knows it; and what he does not know, he cannot seek, since he does not even know what he should look for[2]

Johannes says that Socrates thinks the difficulty through in the doctrine of Recollection (really a Platonic doctrine), which regards human reason (*logos*) as a reflection of the *logos* of the *cosmos.*

Through dialogue, i.e., through question and answer, the accidental and temporal expressions fall away, and the Truth is "recol-
lected." Thus, "Truth is not introduced into the individual from
without, but was [always] within him."[3] The task of the teacher,
therefore, is to be a midwife: not to impart the Truth but to help
in its delivery. In the Socratic view, the maieutic[4] relationship is
the highest possible between man and man.

From this standpoint, every point of departure is accidental; so
also is the teacher. For example, whoever has grasped the truth of
the proposition that two triangles are congruent if two of their sides
and the included angle are equal, has no longer any need of the
teacher, nor is the occasion of the insight of intrinsic significance.
The teacher could have been anyone; the occasion, likewise, any
time or any place. The truth that has been learned was there, waiting to be *discovered*, and it is independent of both occasion and
teacher.

> If this is what it means to learn the Truth, the fact that I have been
> instructed by Socrates or by Prodicus or by a servant-girl, can con-
> cern me only historically; or so far as I am a Plato in sentimental
> enthusiasm, it may concern me poetically. . . . Nor can it interest
> me otherwise than historically that Socrates' or Prodicus' doctrine
> was this or that; for the Truth in which I rest was within me, and
> came to light through myself, and not even Socrates could have given
> it to me. . . . My relation to Socrates or Prodicus cannot concern me
> with respect to my eternal happiness,[5] for this was given me retro-
> gressively through my possession of the Truth, which I had from the
> beginning without knowing it.[6]

This, in short compass, is Johannes' first point, one answer to the
question, "How far does the Truth admit of being learned?" He
then proceeds to examine an alternative.

> Now if the situation is to be otherwise, then the Moment in time
> must have a decisive significance, so that I will never be able to for-
> get it either in time or eternity, because the Eternal, which hitherto
> did not exist, came into existence in this moment.[7] On the basis of
> this presupposition let us now consider the implications of the ques-
> tion as to how far the truth can be learned.[8]

Here Johannes begins a chain of reasoning in which the implications of the Moment as having decisive significance for the individual (henceforth called 'the believer') are deduced from this hypothesis. The argument is too closely worked to be summarized easily, but what in fact results by the neatest of logic is all of Christian doctrine, though without explicit reference to Christ. Since the Truth comes into existence in the historical Moment, the learner, up to the time he receives it, must have been without it and therefore in error. The Teacher, rather than serving as the occasion for his remembering the Truth, must bring it to him. But this can be done only by God, hence the Teacher must be himself God. And what about the error in which the individual has stood? "Let us call it *Sin*."[9] In this manner (much abbreviated in this capsule summary), the reasoning unfolds. There is no alternative to reading Johannes' own argument if one would savor its full flavor. From the initial hypothesis that the Moment have a decisive significance, one doctrine flows from another with a logical cogency that is at once slick and impressive.

Commentators have not been slow to point out the similarity between this argument in *Fragments* and Anselm's rational argument for the Incarnation in *Cur Deus Homo*. In his Commentary on *Fragments*, Niels Thulstrup summarizes Anselm's argument in this way: "The logical and metaphysical necessity of the Incarnation is maintained, because God's righteousness requires either punishment or satisfaction for man's sin. If man were to be punished as he deserves, God's eternal resolution of salvation could not be fulfilled—therefore satisfaction must be made. Man ought to make this satisfaction, but is unable to. God alone is able to do this, and therefore God became man: *nemo potest nisi Deus, nemo debet nisi homo, ergo Deus homo*."[10]

The parallel is certainly striking, but there is an equally striking difference between Anselm and Johannes, as well as between Anselm and Thulstrup. Let us start with this latter difference. Anselm qualified his rational argument with the proviso that *if* God willed to save the world, then reason requires that he would have to do it by becoming incarnate in a man—the mystery of God and man as one in Christ. As a representative of the high Middle Ages, Anselm displayed a courageous use of reason that was in considerable degree informed by the Socratic perspective to which we have alluded. While Anselm was clearly convinced of the rational character of Christian doctrine, he never supposed that it was rationally necessary that God should *will* to save the world. That was

31

grace. The Incarnation as such was not necessary; only its rational character. Here lies a difference between Anselm and Thulstrup.

With respect to Johannes, the difference is equally great. For him, the premise that the Moment have decisive significance is neither rationally necessary nor a matter of grace. It is merely an interesting hypothesis, the implications of which it amuses him to work out. We are forewarned of this in the Preface, where he states that he is an idler from love of ease and by inclination. This "Project of Thought," as he calls it at the beginning of chapter 1, is undertaken for his own entertainment. "But what is my opinion [of the matters discussed in the book]? . . . Don't ask me about that; beyond whether I have any opinion or not, nothing could very well be of less importance to another than what my opinion is."[11] And if these disclaimers are insufficient to warn the reader that he is not about to embark upon an existentially serious piece of writing, Johannes inserted between the Preface and chapter 1 a "Proposition," which reads:

Propositio
The question is asked in ignorance
by one who does not even know
what can have led him to ask in this way.

The question, let it be emphasized again, is how far the Truth by which one can live one's life authentically, fulfill one's true destiny, admits of being learned. What concerns every man or woman, unconditionally, is treated by Johannes as an entertaining hypothesis, the implications of which he develops in order to while away the time. Nothing could be further from Anselm, for whom the event of Jesus as the Christ—the moment in history that is decisive for the life of every believer—is evidence of God's grace mediated through the Church and received by faith.

One thing is very clear: *Philosophical Fragments* cannot have been written by a Christian. The experimental hypothesis, viz., *if* the moment is to have decisive significance, i.e., *if* Jesus is the Christ, . . . is incompatible with the fundamental Christian confession that Jesus is Lord. The "if" makes it clear at the outset that what Johannes is undertaking is but a project of thought, an intellectual game, with no other purpose than to entertain in the way in which any exercise of logic or mathematics might prove amusing. The non-Christian character of the book is further suggested by Johannes' use of the definite article in referring to God. He speaks not of God [*Gud*] but of the God [*Guden*], a usage that underscores the speculative distance he maintains from the deity about which he writes.

In the remaining chapters of the book, Johannes raises many interesting questions and deals with them in a highly creative way; one cannot gainsay the fact that his reflections shed light on important religious issues. This is characteristic of Kierkegaard's pseudonymous writings. In them he deals with Christian themes, and he deals with them insightfully, but when the pseudonymous author has had his say, the result is a document that is not Christian at all. The basic presuppositions underlying the pseudonymous works are aesthetical. *Fragments* manifests only a dilettante's passing interest, not a believer's unconditional concern. To use Josiah Thompson's phrase, the pseudonyms' writings ring false to the core.

The second chapter is entitled, "God as Teacher and Saviour." The subtitle points to its aesthetic character: "An Essay of the Imagination." Arguing that the God is moved by love to rescue the one in error, Johannes imagines the staggering difficulty that such an undertaking poses for the God. Since there is an absolute unlikeness between the God and man, how can the God come into a relationship with man without thereby annihilating that unlikeness and thus failing to reveal *Himself*? To illuminate the difficulty, Johannes tells (creates) a story of a powerful king who loved a humble maiden and would marry her. Then there awakens in the heart of the king an anxious thought: were he to marry her, could she forget that he was a great king and she but a humble maiden? "Even if the maiden would be content to become as nothing, this could not satisfy the king, precisely because he loved her, and because it was harder for him to be her benefactor than to lose her. And suppose she could not even understand him?"[12] Translating this back into the problem which the God has with respect to the one in error, Johannes points out that the God loves the sinner, although the latter does not love Him and is happy in his fate. Now follows a characteristic Johannine passage, which I cannot resist quoting in full.

Our problem is now before us, and we invite the poet,[13] if he is not already invited elsewhere, or if he is not a person who has to be chased out of the house of mourning, together with the flute-players and other noise-makers, if gladness is to come in, [to help us].[14] The poet's task will be to find a solution, a point of unity, where love's understanding truly is, where the God's anxiety has its pain overcome. For the divine love is that unfathomable love which cannot rest content with that which the beloved might in his folly prize as blessedness.[15]

The passage is beautiful, but the irony is pervasive. The poet must find a solution to the God's difficulty, so that the God's anxiety can be set at rest, and solve the problem of salvation. The poet must come to the God's rescue! In this case, of course, the poet is Johannes Climacus. The tone of the paragraph, like its content, is almost frivolous, treating the mystery of the Incarnation as though it were a puzzle for some wise wit to solve, without, of course, acknowledging what he is doing. Christianity's divine mystery is reduced to a project of idle but clever thought. Again, Kierkegaard is presenting the aesthetical standpoint in its cold, cynical purity, barely disguised as religious concern.

Subsequent chapters deal with such topics as the problem of the existence of God (a brilliant treatment), the absolute paradox, which is the Moment when the eternal enters time,[16] and, finally, the nature of the relationship of the believer (the disciple) to the historical event that is at the same time the Moment. These are all, obviously, issues with which the philosophy of religion and Christian theology must deal, and Johannes deals with them insightfully, so much so that one is continually tempted to suppose that Johannes is really a concerned believer. It is a temptation to which one should not yield, however, for the price of forgetting Johannes' basic presuppositions is to miss the irony and so to miss the point.

That point was Kierkegaard's purpose in writing the book. He wanted, by use of irony, to show that any attempt to explain the mystery of divine grace, the mystery of God's love for his lost children, is to engage in a curious inversion. One created God in one's own image, the image of a clever solver of problems, rather than accepting, with understanding informed by faith, the grace that is offered in Jesus Christ. Kierkegaard was no anti-intellectual; on the contrary, he was a prototypal intellectual. His life was in large measure a life of thought, but he knew that thought is no substitute for faith, and that reason without faith becomes idolatrous. *Fragments* is an aesthetical work, a work of irony, aimed at those who would substitute thinking about religion for the reality of faith.

34

At the conclusion of *Fragments* Johannes admits that he has dealt with Christian themes without seeming to do so, and he hints about writing another section of the work.

> If I ever write [another] section, it is my intention to call the subject by its right name, and to clothe the problem in its historical costume.[17] If I ever write a next section—for an author of pieces such as I, as you will, I suppose, hear about me, has no seriousness of purpose; how then should I now in conclusion feign a seriousness I do not have? . . . What the historical costume of the following section will be is not hard to see. It is well known that Christianity is the only historical phenomenon which in spite of the historical, nay precisely by means of the historical, has intended itself to be for the single individual the point of departure of his eternal consciousness, has intended to interest him otherwise than merely historically, has intended to base his eternal blessedness on his relationship to something historical.[18]

In the "next section," then, the problem will be "clothed in its historical costume," Christianity; but Johannes is careful to warn the reader anew that he has no seriousness of purpose in doing this. The problem is pursued solely because it interests him. His work is not a reflection by a man of faith upon the significance of the event of Jesus as the Christ. On the contrary, his personal "thought experiment" is now to be clad in traditional costume in order to see what further implications can be deduced from the original hypothesis. It is his interest in that hypothesis, not the claim of Christ upon him, that determines the nature of his investigations.

The next section did in fact appear and turned out to be a huge volume, far larger than the slight volume to which it is ironically called a postscript; and while the problem is clothed as promised in its Christian costume, its treatment reveals no change of standpoint or of heart in the aesthete who is its author. Its English title, *Concluding Unscientific Postscript*, renders the Danish original somewhat unclearly. The word that is translated by "unscientific" [*uvidenskabelig*] can equally well be rendered by "unscholarly."[19] I myself would prefer "unscholarly" in the title, but Swenson's original choice cannot now be reversed. Kierkegaard obviously wished to disassociate Johannes Climacus, with his humorous and aesthetic detachment, from the serious scholars, particularly the

Hegelian theologians, whom he was attacking. Their "seriousness" evoked his scorn, because they seriously believed that they could legitimize Christianity by rational argument.

The *Postscript* undertakes, naturally enough, to enlarge upon the basic issue raised in *Fragments*, viz., the paradox—the hypothesis that the Moment in time shall have a decisive significance for the individual's eternal blessedness. As promised, Johannes clothes the matter in its Christian costume. Referring to *Fragments* he writes,

> The problem that was set forth in that piece, though without pretence of having solved it, since the intention was only to pose it, was as follows: *Can there be an historical point of departure for an eternal consciousness; how can this have more than historical interest; can an eternal blessedness be based on some historical knowledge?*[20]

It is well known, Johannes argues, that Christianity makes such claims. "I have heard that Christianity proposes itself as a necessary condition for the attainment of this good [i.e., eternal blessedness]; now I ask, how do I establish a relationship to this doctrine?"[21]

Johannes thus discloses at the outset his fundamental misunderstanding of Christianity, at least in its authentic form.[22] Christianity does not propose *itself* as a condition of salvation. That would be idolatrous. It does indeed affirm that Jesus is the Christ, that "the Word became flesh and dwelt among us, full of grace and truth," and that it is the mission of the Church to proclaim this good news; but Christianity does not set itself up as the necessary condition for receiving God's grace.[23]

Furthermore, from a Christian perspective, the issue is not how one can establish a proper relationship to a doctrine but how one comes into a proper relationship with God and one's neighbor.[24] Kierkegaard dealt with the centrality of love in Christian life in one of his finest Christian books, *Works of Love*, which we shall consider in the next chapter. In contrast, Johannes, as a spectator of life, standing as best he can apart from it, uninvolved save for his idle interest in the intellectual puzzle that captivates him for the time being, inevitably understands Christianity from outside which is to say, he misunderstands it in a fundamental way. Like *Fragments*, the *Postscript* is an intellectual experiment, and Johannes' view of Christianity conforms to the experiment and not to the historic Christian witness. Johannes confesses as much toward the end of the book: "That an eternal blessedness is decided in time through the relationship to something historical was the content of *my experiment and what I now call Christianity* [emphasis mine]."[25] His understanding of his experiment provides the criterion of what Christianity is presumed to be.

The experimental, hypothetical nature of Johannes' project is emphasized often, as when he says again toward the close of the *Postscript*, "Only let me again repeat: I do not attempt to decide whether Christianity is right or wrong. My bit of merit, if any, consists in presenting the problem," i.e., the paradox of the Moment in time, and how one is to be related to it.[26] This is asserted also at the beginning of the book.

> Without having understood Christianity, since I merely present the problem, I have though understood this much: that it will bestow upon the individual an eternal blessedness, thus presupposing in the individual an infinite interest in his eternal blessedness as a *conditio sine qua non*. . . . Although I am only an outsider, I have at least understood this much, that the only unpardonable offense against the majesty of Christianity is for the individual to take his relationship to it for granted, treating it as a matter of course."[27]

We note once more that the source of eternal blessedness is Christianity, not God or Christ; one must not sin against its majesty. Here again the idolatrous character of Johannes' project is disclosed. One must acknowledge, however, that, as is so often the case with the pseudonyms, he has important insights as well as a pervasive misunderstanding—near misses one might call them. As has already been observed, what makes the positions of the pseudonyms so persuasive is that they often articulate Christian insights, albeit from a fundamentally unchristian point of view.

What, then, is the problem with which the book is concerned? Briefly stated, it is this: If the historical Moment has decisive significance for the individual, how can he appropriate its truth? To illuminate this problem, Johannes must first develop the distinction between truth as objectivity and truth as subjectivity, together with the implications of this distinction.

> The objective problem would then be: the truth of Christianity. The subjective problem is: the relationship of the individual to Christianity. To put it simply: How I, Johannes Climacus, can participate in the blessedness promised by Christianity.[28]

37

If one would consider the truth of Christianity in an objective way, one must ask both its historical truth and its philosophical truth. This, Johannes undertakes to do in Book I, after pointing out that in this kind of undertaking the inquiring subject is not infinitely and personally and passionately interested in his own eternal blessedness. Objectivity implies distance—a disinterested, speculative perspective. Such an inquiry has its own legitimacy, but it cannot discover Christian truth as a matter of passionate concern.

One is here reminded of Buber's distinction between the two primary words, I-it and I-Thou: when one "utters" the primary word I-it, i.e., when one assumes a speculative attitude, he stands outside of what is being investigated. Faith, Johannes rightly sees, implies that one is "infinitely interested" in the source of his eternal blessedness. But it should be noted once again that, for Johannes, Christian faith is an infinite interest in Christianity, not in Christ.[29] It should also be noted that Johannes uses the word "interest," which is regularly used by "A" in *Either/Or.* The aesthete may indeed have a great, even an infinite interest in something, but as an *interest* it is nonetheless always temporary, subject to the assaults of boredom. There is an important difference between an infinite interest and what Paul Tillich calls ultimate concern, and that difference is staying power—absolute commitment. Absolute commitment is not to be found in the pseudonymous works; the pseudonyms never rise above interest, however passionate that interest may be.

It follows then that, for Johannes, faith is a *passionate* interest in the truth, and that is precisely the essence of truth as subjectivity.

> Thus Christianity protests against all objectivity; it would have the subject concern itself infinitely with itself. What it asks about is subjectivity; it is in this that Christianity's truth lies, if there is any at all. Objectively it has none whatever.[30]

As Johannes sees the matter, Christianity's truth is to be found in the relationship of the believer to God, not in any objectively established truth. The objective stance, which makes everyone an observer,[31] will never make anyone a Christian. That requires subjectivity—an infinite interest in Christianity (sic), by which one can appropriate it personally. "To become subjective is a highly prized task, which is sufficient for a human life."[32] This is Johannes' thesis.

> For objective reflection truth becomes an object, something objective; the point is that one looks away from the subject. For subjective reflection truth becomes a matter of appropriation, of inwardness, of subjectivity, and here the point is for the existing individual to become immersed in subjectivity. (p. 171)

> The way of objective reflection makes the subject accidental, and thereby transforms existence into something indifferent, something vanishing. (p. 173)

> Subjective reflection turns inward toward the subjectivity and in this intensification [of inwardness] wills to realize the truth, and in such wise that just as in the foregoing, when objectivity was emphasized, subjectivity vanished, here subjectivity itself is the last, and the objective is what vanishes. (p. 175)[33]

Simply put, the speculative or objective approach to truth implies a distance between the subject and the truth. If the truth at issue is the truth by which alone one can live an authentic existence, without whose personal appropriation life is devoid of reality, and existence is without substance, then the speculative philosopher is alienated from his own existence, does not *as philosopher* exist as an infinitely interested subject. This means that without subjectivity, a Christian is one in name only.

It is worth noting at this point that Johannes, for all of his praise of truth as subjectivity, does not himself manage to achieve it nor, in fact, does he intend to. In a longish passage[34] which precedes this initial consideration of truth as subjectivity, Johannes tells how he came to undertake the project in which he is now engaged. Given for years to idle thinking, the thought one day flashed through his mind that he might make reflection a bit harder for some of those who followed the easy path of Hegelian philosophy. This was an entertaining prospect, too interesting to resist, and so he decided to undertake it. Again Kierkegaard's irony presents itself: Johannes the idler, passionately advocating truth as subjectivity, but without the least intention of subjectively appropriating the truth for himself. Such absence of inwardness he himself calls madness.[35] Again it must be said: Johannes Climacus is not Kierkegaard.

That subjectivity, or inwardness, is truth, is Johannes' thesis. What is critically important for any individual is that which has significance for his existence as a self, and this because what concerns us unconditionally, what "interests us infinitely," is our self. Passion is stirred where our life and its concerns are at issue. Johannes points out that subjectivity entails passion; it implies an infinite interest in the object, an interest which is lost in the attitude of objectivity. "By forgetting that one is an existing subject, passion goes by the board, and the truth in turn does not become a paradox; the knowing subject becomes a fantastic entity rather than a human being, and truth becomes for it a fantastic object."[36]

Subjective truth is a paradox, because its truth is objectively always uncertain. In common parlance, the phrase "subjective truth" is a contradiction in terms. We scientifically-minded souls are persuaded that the more objective our stance, the greater is the likelihood of our achieving reliable knowledge. Subjectivity, on the other hand, carries with it the stigma of wishful thinking. Undoubtedly there is good ground for this. For example, it is impossible to live without trusting others, yet there is no way *objectively* to establish their trustworthiness. No matter how trustworthily a person acts, it is impossible both to be certain that his action is not deception and to justify one's trust in him. One need only engage in a bit of self-reflection to realize with what ease dishonesty can be passed off as trustworthiness. Like love, trust entails risk; its validity cannot be certified objectively, but where it exists, it nevertheless carries with it the absolute conviction of truth. This kind of subjective conviction stands in paradoxical opposition to trust's objective uncertainty.

Johannes summarizes his discussion as follows:

> When the question of truth is raised objectively, reflection is directed toward truth as an object to which the knower relates himself. Reflection is not upon the relationship but upon whether it is truth, what is true, to which the knower relates himself. When that to which he relates himself is the truth, the true, then the subject is in the truth. When the question of truth is raised subjectively, reflection is directed subjectively to the nature of the individual's relationship [to it]; if only the mode of this relationship is in the truth, then the individual is in the truth, even if he should relate himself to what is [objectively] untrue.[37]

To this statement Johannes adds a footnote: "The reader will observe that the question here is about essential truth, or about the truth which is essentially related to existence, and that it is precisely for the sake of clarifying it as inwardness or as subjectivity that this contrast is drawn."

Johannes further points out that, since God is a subject, he exists only for subjectivity; he cannot be brought to light objectively. Nor can Jesus be recognized as the Christ by any conceivable objective study. In an oft cited passage, Johannes gives this description of truth as subjectivity: *"The objectively uncertain that is adhered to and appropriated with the most passionate inwardness is the truth,* the highest truth attainable for an *existing* individual."[38] The relevance of Johannes' view for the Christian's faith in the incarnation of Christ is obvious. No unambiguous signs attest to Christ's divinity; indeed, his suffering and death upon the cross appear to contradict this claim. He was admittedly an important historical figure and rightfully has his place in history along with many others. So regarded, Jesus' place in history is relative. For the Christian, however, he is the Word become flesh; but this is a truth given only in subjectivity. Thus, the eternal and essential truth is a paradox which can be grasped only through the risk of faith.

> Without risk there is no faith. Faith is precisely the contradiction between the infinite passion of inwardness and objective uncertainty. If I can grasp God objectively, then I do not believe, but precisely because I cannot do that, I must believe. If I would preserve myself in faith, I must constantly watch out that I hold fast to that objective uncertainty, that in that objective uncertainty I am "in over 70,000 fathoms of water," and yet I believe.[39]

Johannes has distinguished cogently between truth as objectivity and truth as subjectivity. There can be no doubt that an objective relationship to the truth, such as that which characterizes science, will never yield faith. Faith entails passion, commitment, "infinite interest" (i.e., ultimate concern). But an existential relationship to the truth, which characterizes *Christian faith,* is not necessarily the same as truth as subjectivity. The endless variety of fanaticisms—racism, Hitlerism, chauvinism, nationalism—conforms nicely to Johannes' view of truth as subjectivity. When, speaking of the existence of God, he says, "Objectively, reflection is upon whether the object is the true God; subjectively, upon whether the individual is related to something *in such a manner* that his relationship is in truth a God-relationship,"[40] it is clear that he has not defended himself against the charge that truth as subjectivity is compatible with the omnipresence of polytheism in human existence. Truth as subjectivity is the essence of all fanaticism and idolatry. In idolatry the relationship of the individual to the god (one should not say "idol," because for the idolatrous individual the object of worship is always god and not idol) is faith. Only if one implicitly and unconsciously assumes that the "objectively uncertain" is not uncertain but is indeed the presence of the divine in history and, therefore, objectively the truth, can one claim that its passionate appropriation subjectively gives true definition and substance to the believer's existence. The contradiction in this is, of course, self-evident.

It follows that the truth of the Incarnation cannot be established objectively, *nor will its subjective appropriation disclose its truth.* Johannes understands the former but not the latter. He fails to lize—or at least to admit—that truth, as subjectivity, is the essence of all fanaticism and idolatry.

For faith, on the other hand, Jesus of Nazareth is indeed the Christ, but faith does not and cannot transmute Jesus of Nazareth into the Christ. Christianly understood, the believer believes by the grace of God—by the power of the Holy Spirit—that Jesus is the Word made flesh, and no philosophical or theological argumentation can either prove or disclose this. It is no accident that Johannes, who does not believe, leaves the reader suspended between equally untenable alternatives: truth as objectivity and truth as subjectivity. While he argues for the latter, he cannot himself participate in it. He is engaged in a thought experiment, and that Christianity is the truth, is something that he cannot himself decide. One must add, of course, that for the Christian, Christianity is not the truth: Christ is the way, the truth, and the life. Johannes does not get beyond Christianity and its alleged claims. The mystery of the Incarnation, of divine grace, eludes him.

Johannes' exposition of truth as subjectivity is one source of Sartre's contention that the individual chooses his values and, by that choice, brings them into existence. (Judge William is another.) Sartre, not some new version of Christian theology, is the actual beneficiary of Climacus' project of thought. One may wonder why so many have accepted his thought experiment as a serious statement of Christian belief. The answer lies in part, at least, in the genius of Kierkegaard, who was careful always to make his pseudonyms speak persuasively to those who mistakenly thought they were Christians and yet, at the same time, to present a position which ironically denied the essence of being a Christian: faith through grace. Just as Johannes de silentio regards faith as self-contradictory movements that he can neither understand nor perform, so Johannes Climacus identifies faith with subjectivity, which is not wrong but is certainly not Christian. While it is clear that faith without subjective passion is dead, it does not follow that subjective passion *is* faith—at least not Christian faith. Christian faith is a response to the grace of God in Jesus Christ. No philosophical analysis will lead to it nor capture its essence. In describing truth as subjectivity, which was his thesis, Johannes succeeds in describing an element common both to idolatry and to Christian faith, but he fails necessarily to touch upon or point to the decisive element in Christian faith: the miracle of God's grace. This is what Anselm understood and what Thulstrup missed and what Johannes ignores.[41] Johannes fails to point to God's grace, for the simple reason that he is not a Christian. He is engaged not in theological reflection but in a thought experiment. His fundamental presuppositions exclude the possibility that his position can be Christian.

In sum, Kierkegaard has presented an author who would offer an alternative to the sterile position of Denmark's Hegelian theologians, but the alternative proves to be a subtle invitation to idolatry, as both Sartre and Camus have made clear. *Truth as objectivity and truth as subjectivity are equally removed from Christian truth—from the miracle of grace that is received through faith in Christ.* It was Kierkegaard's hope that, after an initial enchantment with Johannes' thesis, his reader would perceive its demonic character and would realize that one cannot think one's way into the Kingdom of God. Neither objective truth nor subjective truth can be identified with the miracle of divine grace.

History's verdict on Kierkegaard's endeavor would appear to be negative. He overestimated the subtlety of many of his readers, who have been convinced that Johannes' heresy is a new contribution to Christian thought. This is the more surprising in view of the final chapter, "Appendix: For an Understanding with the Reader," in which Johannes again affirms that he is not a Christian but a humorist. He explains that he has written the book for himself alone, that it is entirely without authority, and that anyone who appeals to it as an authority has, in so doing, misunderstood it. Having no opinion except one, namely that it must be the most difficult of all things to become a Christian ("which opinion is no opinion and possesses none of the qualities which usually characterize 'an opinion' "), he asserts:

> I have no opinion and wish to have none, being content and pleased with this. As in Catholic books, especially those of an earlier age, one finds at the back of the volume a note which informs the reader that everything is to be understood conformably with the doctrine of the Holy Catholic Mother Church, so what I write contains also a piece of information to the effect that everything is so to be understood that it is understood to be revoked, and the book has not only a conclusion but into the bargain a revocation. More than that no one can require, either before or after.[42]

With this ironic disclaimer Johannes concludes his ponderous postscript to the *Fragments*. A Christian he is not, a theologian he is not. Johannes is precisely what he says he is: a humorist, who is intrigued but not claimed by the question of how one can become a Christian, which he acknowledges is undoubtedly the most difficult of all things.

CHAPTER FOUR

Irony, melancholy and Christianity were, as previously noted, formative factors in Kierkegaard's work as an author. But certain persistent themes also inform his writings, themes which are basic to human existence. Despair and love are two of these, and they constantly claimed Kierkegaard's attention. Despair, which we shall deal with in the next chapter, permeates the aestheticism of "A" and has no more forceful expression than in his opening words in *Either/Or*.

> What is a poet? A poet is an unhappy being, who hides deep torments in his heart, but whose lips are so formed that as the sighs and cries escape them, they sound like beautiful music . . .[1]

A despairing cynicism runs throughout Volume 1. "A," as Judge William repeatedly observes, is in despair. But it is by no means clear that Judge William escapes that condition, nor indeed any human being.

Kierkegaard's preoccupation with despair is in part, of course, a reflection of his melancholy; but more important, it is also an expression of his Christian faith. For despair is the psychological aspect of sin. *The Sickness unto Death* contains a profound psychological analysis of despair as well as a deeply Christian interpretation of it—despair as an essential element of sin. In our consideration of that book (in the next chapter), which is one of his most important Christian writings, we shall compare the analysis which he makes there with the concept of despair found in *Either/Or*.

Love also occupied a central place in Kierkegaard's writing, which is hardly surprising in view of the fact that his tortured romance with Regine Olsen was the painful occasion of his early pseudonymous writings. As is true of his treatment of despair, his reflections on love range from the cynical eroticism of Johannes the Seducer to the sublimity of his description of Christian love in *Works of Love*. It is instructive to compare the views of love found in *Works of Love* and in *Either/Or*. But first we must have a look at the central thesis of *Works of Love*.

In 1930 the first volume of Anders Nygren's important work, *Eros and Agape*, was published. It was soon translated into many languages and had an enormous influence in theological circles. The central theme of the book was the exploration of the difference between the Greek *eros*, i.e., the love for that with which (or with whom) a person longs to unite himself, and the New Testament's *agape*, i.e., the love which God in Christ has shown mankind and which every individual ought to show his neighbor. It is interesting that in *Works of Love*, which was published in 1847, Kierkegaard had already distinguished between these two meanings of the word "love." Moreover, he had in addition underscored his contemporaries' proneness to confuse the two and to let them blend together, thus making the word "love" ambiguous and often misleading.

When one reads *Works of Love*, one moves in an atmosphere entirely different from that of the pseudonymous works. The irony of the pseudonyms is absent. In this book Kierkegaard speaks directly to his reader about the Gospel's demands and blessing. Those who find the pseudonymous works confusing and contrivedly cunning are immediately struck by Kierkegaard's straightforward and passionate exposition of love's demand and fruit in human life. As is true of all of his books, his aesthetic artistry gives exquisite form to his prose; but what is central and important is his Christian purpose. Love's nature is clarified, love is praised—and all to the glory of God. In addition, the reader is invited to reflect upon his own life and to consider anew God's command to him. *Works of Love* is an appeal for self-examination; it is to be read as though it speaks solely to *me* about *my* life.

In keeping with the book's character, Kierkegaard begins *Works of Love* with a prayer, of which the opening words are:

> How could love be rightly spoken of if you, Lord, were forgotten— you God of love, source of all love in heaven and on earth, you who spared nothing but gave all in love, you who are love, so that he who loves is what he is only by being in you! How could love be rightly spoken of if you were forgotten—you who revealed what love is, you our saviour and redeemer, who gave yourself to save all! How could love be rightly spoken of if you were forgotten—you who are the spirit of love, you who take nothing for your own but remind us of love's sacrifice, remind the believer to love as he is loved, and his neighbor as himself![2]

This prayer, in characteristically trinitarian form, reveals Kierkegaard's profoundly held Christian convictions. If one will speak truly of love, one must acknowledge God's presence, for love is of God. If one will speak truly of love, then one must speak of its divine yet hidden source.

> As God dwells in a light from which streams every beam which lights the world, and yet no one can penetrate back by these paths to see God, for the light's paths change to darkness when one turns toward the light: so love dwells in the hidden, is hidden in the inmost depths.[3]

When for any reason a person forgets or fails to realize that God is the source of all love in heaven and on earth, then he falls into error and calls what is really self-love by the name of love as, for example, when a person loudly asseverates that he cannot live without the beloved "but will hear nothing of love's task and demand . . . [but will call] by the name of love what is simply a weak indulgence . . . or a selfish relationship."[4] We must not deceive ourselves about love, says Kierkegaard; that is the most terrible thing we can do. But this is, of course, something that can and does happen. We become totally involved with our own feelings and desires and preferences, and we assume that in these emotional relationships with others such feelings are love. In this way, says Kierkegaard, we lose love's blessing.

Love is at the core of life, hidden in its depths. In a famous passage Kierkegaard writes,

The hidden life of love is, in the most inward depths, unfathomable, and then again has an unfathomable connection with the whole of existence. As a quiet lake is fed deep down by the flow of hidden springs, which no eye sees, so a human being's love is grounded, still more deeply, in God's love. If there were no spring at the bottom, if God were not love, then there would be neither the little lake nor human love. As the quiet lake has its source obscurely in the deep spring, so the individual's love is grounded mysteriously in God's love. As the quiet lake invites you to contemplate it but the reflected image of the dark depths prevents you from seeing through it, so love's mysterious origin in God's love prevents you from seeing its source. When you think you are seeing it, you are deceived by a reflection, as if it were the bottom—this which only conceals the deeper bottom.[5]

No one can see love. There are no deeds that constitute unambiguous evidence of its presence. So-called "good works"[6] are not in themselves a sign of love. A person can give alms and yet be motivated solely by pride, or be friendly toward others in order more easily to use them. It is thus possible to act so as to give the appearance of love, but in reality to love only oneself. Love is of God. Its source is therefore hidden, and it is known only by its fruits. We love truly, says Kierkegaard, only when we love the one whom God loves—our neighbor. True love has its source in God's love, which alone moves our hearts to care for others, quite apart from our feelings toward them. In contrast, immature and deceitful love is readily recognizable, because it amounts to no more than vain protestations.

In all of this Kierkegaard reflects Luther's attack on justification by good works. For Kierkegaard, as for Luther, there are no special words, no special deeds, which in themselves show that a person acts from love and accepts others in love.

There is no deed, not a single one, not even the best, of which we dare to say unconditionally: he who does this thereby unconditionally demonstrates love. It depends on *how* the deed is done. There are indeed acts which in a special sense are called works of love (good works). But truly, because one makes charitable contributions, because one visits the widow and clothes the naked, one's love is still not thereby demonstrated or made recognizable, for one can perform works of love [*kjerlighedsgerninger*] in an unloving, yes, even in a self-loving way, and when this is so, the works of love are nevertheless not love's works [*kjerlighedens gerninger*].[7]

Whether or not our deeds are truly love's works depends upon their source, upon what actually moves us. They are love's works only if the Spirit of God moves our hearts.

The important difference between genuine love and pretend love must be further clarified. Kierkegaard begins his analysis of love's demand with the familiar commandment: you shall love your neighbor as yourself. As yourself. This is the important phrase, he argues, for it presupposes that every human being loves himself and, as a consequence of this, knows full well what the commandment requires. When we refuse to accept love's demand upon us and excuse ourselves by saying we don't rightly understand what it means to love our neighbor, we immediately run head on into the commandment's words, "as yourself."

Everyone knows that he loves himself, that when the chips are down, he will protect his unalienable right to be acknowledged and accepted as a person—as a human being. This touches all of us deeply. When another makes fun of me or does me wrong or snubs me, I am hurt, offended; my feelings are injured, and my being as a person is denied. In a real sense, my selfhood is crushed and negated. Another person *ought* to treat me as a person, acknowledge my right to be myself, accept me for what I am—his neighbor. In fact he ought to *be* my neighbor. This does not mean that the other person is obliged to like me or to be my friend. He is under no obligation to have warm feelings toward me and to invite me to dinner once in a while. But he ought to love me, i.e., he should treat me as the person I am and thus be a neighbor to me. I know that I deserve that, not because I am especially good or clever or important, but solely because I, despite all my faults and imperfections, am nonetheless a human being, a person in my own right. In the final analysis others ought to love me as I love myself—as a human being.

Such are the implications of Kierkegaard's view of the commandment's "as yourself." The point must nevertheless be made that the commandment requires that one shall love oneself in the right way, i.e., as a person, conscious of one's true humanity; for to love oneself as a human being is identical with love for one's neighbor. Of course, it cannot be said that a person will just naturally love himself in the right way. Deeply aware of the persistence of sin in the life of believers and unbelievers alike, Kierkegaard recognized that every individual is strongly, if unconsciously, inclined to love himself as a god, i.e., as one who rightfully has power over others and therefore may regard and use them as objects—as objects of his erotic love or his anger or his sympathy, or as useful in promoting his interests.

Genuine love is different, for it is an acknowledgment of the humanity of the other, an acknowledgment of the other as neighbor. It is a recognition of his or her claim to be recognized as a person. This is possible only where one assumes the responsibility of being oneself a responsible self. When I relate to another in a genuinely human way, I relate to myself in that same way. It is important, therefore, to recognize that self-love is not necessarily selfish self-love; that is actually a self-contradiction. Of the commandment to love your neighbor as yourself, Kierkegaard observes "that it does not seek to teach a man not to love himself but rather seeks to teach him the right self-love."[8]

Kierkegaard's treatment of love and self-love is well summarized in the following passage:

> The commandment reads thus, "You shall love your neighbor as yourself," but if the command is understood rightly, it also says the opposite: *"You shall love yourself in the right way."* If anyone, therefore, refuses to learn from Christianity how to love himself in the right way, he cannot love his neighbor either. He can perhaps stand by one or more persons 'through thick and thin,' as we say, but this is by no means to love one's neighbor. To love oneself in the right way and to love one's neighbor correspond perfectly to one another; fundamentally they are one and the same thing. When the law's *as yourself* has wrested from you the self-love which Christianity sadly enough must presuppose to be in every man, precisely then have you learned to love yourself. The law is, therefore: you shall love yourself in the same way as you love your neighbor when you love him as yourself.[9]

In Kierkegaard's view, most people, however, love themselves in a selfish way. Their love is preferential love for the beloved, or spontaneous affection or erotic desire.[10] Preferential love can be strong and provisionally faithful, but it is not neighbor love. In preferential love, one loves another (and oneself) not according to the requirements of the law but according to the intensity of one's preference. In friendship and erotic love, the friend or lover will love the chosen one above and to the exclusion of all others, simply because he follows the dictates of his own impulses. The relationship is determined by psychological forces working unconsciously and powerfully. In such relationships the individual puts himself and his beloved ahead of his neighbor. Indeed, preferential love does not recognize the neighbor at all; the beloved is loved not for himself but for his attractiveness, for the pleasure that he gives the lover.

In contrast, Christianity teaches us to love our neighbor—to love all whom we are fond of and all whom we are not fond of, to love all people, even our enemy, and to make no exception, whether dictated by preference or aversion. It teaches us to accept any and all persons *as persons*, regardless of inclination or interest. Preferential love, in contrast to this, elevates the beloved above all others, hence to the status of a god.

> There is only one whom a man can with the truth of the eternal love above himself—that is God. Therefore it is not said: "Thou shalt love God as thyself," but rather, "Thou shalt love the Lord thy God with all thy heart, with all thy soul, and all thy mind."[11]

To love any human being unconditionally is idolatry. And just this, in Kierkegaard's view, is what everyone does by virtue of mankind's sinful nature. Therefore we all have to be *commanded* to love our neighbor, for our natural disposition is to love friend or lover higher than all others and *ipso facto* to ignore both neighbor and God.

But who is my neighbor? This question, with which the parable of the Good Samaritan is introduced, leads Kierkegaard to observe that our neighbor is as near to us as our self-love. If there are two of us, the other is our neighbor. If there are millions, every one of these is our neighbor. And every neighbor is closer than friend or beloved, because these tend to become objects of preference rather than to be what they are: neighbors. My neighbor is the one to whom I have a duty, and when I fulfill my duty, I prove that I am a neighbor.

> Christ does not speak about recognizing one's neighbor but about being a neighbor oneself, about proving oneself to be a neighbor,

something that the Samaritan proved by his compassion; for by that he did not prove that the assaulted man was his neighbor, but that he was a neighbor to the one assaulted. . . . Choosing a lover, finding a friend, yes, that is a long, hard job, but one's neighbor is easy to recognize, easy to find—if one will only acknowledge one's duty."[12]

It is impossible, therefore, not to know who our neighbor is. There is not a single person in the whole world whom it is so easy to recognize as my neighbor, for all people are my neighbor.

If you confuse another man with your neighbor, the mistake does not lie there, for the other man is your neighbor also; the mistake lies in you, that you do not will to understand who your neighbor is. If you save someone's life in the dark, this again is no mistake; alas, it is, on the contrary, a mistake that you only want to save your friend.[13]

This observation brings into sharp focus the radical difference between the Christian understanding of love and that of the pagan,[14] which is hardly to be differentiated from the common understanding of love that obtains in our society today. It is the distinction between love as a disinterested concern for and acceptance of whomever I meet, and love as a preference for those to whom I am attracted erotically or by ties of affection (or admiration or interest). Such attraction is, of course, unavoidable, because it is natural. Kierkegaard remarks that people have generally supposed that Christianity has disdained erotic love, because it is grounded psychologically in impulse. It is certainly obvious that preferential love is a natural passion. For reasons of his or her own psychological nature and personal history, one particular individual will fall in love with another, although a third may be quite unable to understand what either of them sees in the other. Erotic love illustrates the element of the accidental in life. A particular erotic relationship depends upon factors of which the participants as a rule are wholly unconscious. We seldom if ever understand ourselves and what makes us tick. Erotic attraction has its roots deep in the psyche, in unconscious memories or needs. In this respect it is not a matter of choice or decision but of impulse. The attraction simply occurs.[15] Moreover, it is entirely accurate to say of a couple, that they have fallen in love—they quite literally fall into it. Christianity has not taken and should not take a stand against this.

Just as it has not forbidden men to eat and drink, so has it not been scandalized by a drive men have not given themselves.[16]

Kierkegaard was no ascetic; but he was very clear about the danger inherent in preferential love. This manifests itself whenever an individual becomes so overwhelmingly engrossed in his own desires and longings that he has an eye only for his beloved and does not give others a passing thought. It is then that self-love is transmuted into selfishness. If, however, the beloved is accepted as neighbor, if one recognizes in one's beloved or friend a neighbor as well, then the relationship is authentically human.

Thus we are commanded not to use another person for our own enjoyment or benefit, even if that person is our friend or our beloved, even if we are head over heels in love. Of course, we should enjoy those whom we love, but we should be a neighbor to them as well. In short, natural affection or powerful erotic attraction is no excuse for not accepting as persons those with whom we are in love or with whom we have powerful bonds of affection; these persons are neither to be used nor worshiped, but loved and served for their own sakes. In this the love of God is decisive, for God is love's hidden source, and from that source alone arises love to one's neighbor.

Fundamentally love to God is decisive; from this arises love to one's neighbor. . . . Love God above all else and then love your neighbor and in your neighbor every man. Only by loving God above all else can one love his neighbor in the next human being.[17]

While neighbor love and preferential love are radically different, they do not exclude each other. Preference is a fact of life and has its own value. But it must not be permitted to prevent us from showing neighbor love, i.e., true love, to those for whom we feel preferential love.

Go, then, and do this: take away distinction and the like, so that you can love your neighbor. Take away the distinctions of preferential love, so that you can love your neighbor. You are not therefore to cease loving the beloved because of this, far from it. If this were so, the word *neighbor* would be the greatest deceit ever fabricated—if you, in order to love your neighbor, must begin by ceasing to love those for whom you have a preference. Moreover, it would also be a contradiction, for, since your neighbor is all men, then no one can be excluded . . ."[18]

It is possible, Kierkegaard contends, to be a neighbor to someone we love but, in a profound sense, this is more difficult than to show neighbor love to a stranger, because our needs—our need to satisfy desire and our need to worship—elevate the one for whom we have preferential love to an absolute status. Hence we must be *commanded* to love our neighbor. Kierkegaard expresses it in this exhortation:

> Love your beloved faithfully and tenderly, but let love to your neighbor be the sanctifier in your covenant of union with God; love your friend sincerely and devotedly, but let love to your neighbor be what you learn from each other in friendship's intimacy with God![19]

In short, do not forget that your spouse or your friend is, first of all, a human being whom you therefore ought to love as a human being, created by God and and loved by God, and never as a convenience, as a source of satisfaction and happiness, or as an idol.

Like everything that is temporal, preferential love can change and even become its opposite.

> Hate is love which has become its opposite, a love which has gone to ruin. Deep down, love is continually aflame, but it is the flame of hate. Only when love is burned out, is the flame of hate also extinguished. Just as it is said of the tongue, that "It is the same tongue with which we bless and curse," so may one also say that it is the same love which loves and hates.[20]

Romantic love is vulnerable to disappointments and irritations, to jealousy and the collapse of expectations (as when, for example, one partner discovers that the other is not the person one had supposed) and to the countless other difficulties that beset all human relationships. It is all too readily transmuted into hate. Those who are sentimentally inclined will likely prefer to believe that it is easy to fall in love with another, and in a way that is quite true. In reality, though, what is easiest of all is to fall in love with one's own dreams. A woman, for example, may project her unconscious hopes and needs on the man to whom she is attracted, completely unaware of why she loves him. When, in time, she becomes disappointed, because he will not, indeed cannot become the content of those dreams, she becomes angry and, finally, ends up hating the man she loves. To hate whom you love is, of course, a contradiction, but contradictory impulses rule the human soul, which in Kierkegaard's view are evidence of sin.

Against this stands the commandment. While spontaneous love is fickle, duty is firm. Only when love has undergone eternity's transformation by becoming duty has it won stability. This means that he who acknowledges his duty to love his neighbor will do so in spite of his selfish inclinations: "Only when it is a duty to love, only then is love eternally and happily secured against despair."[21]

To contemporary ears it may sound peculiar to speak of a duty to love. Nowadays, the majority believe that the greatest bliss is to fall in love with "the one and only" and to live happily ever after. How can we speak of a duty to fall in love? That is something that simply happens—when and if it happens. In reply it must, of course, be acknowledged that we have no duty to fall in love. But we have a duty to love our neighbor, because we have a duty to love God and ourselves. This is Kierkegaard's meaning. Neighbor love is a response to the claim which another person makes upon us by virtue of being a human being and so the object of God's love. Against the insistent claims of preference sounds the voice of duty: you shall love your neighbor as yourself. Only the voice of duty will free men from the depersonalizing pressures of spontaneous love and introduce a measure of realism in human relationships.

> When it is a duty to love those we see, then we must first and foremost give up all fanciful and extravagant notions about a dreamworld where the object of love is to be sought and found; that is, one must become sober, win actuality and truth by finding and remaining in the world of actuality as one's assigned task . . .
>
> When in loving it is a duty to love the persons we see, then what is at issue is that in loving an actual individual person one does not slip in an imagined notion about what one thinks or could wish this person should be.[22]

It may appear that for Kierkegaard the Christian message about love is finally a new law: it is your duty to love your neighbor. In this, however, he is not contradicting the New Testament message, for Jesus said, "You shall love your neighbor as yourself." Kierkegaard's understanding of the relationship of the Gospel and duty is well expressed in the conclusion of the book:

> In the foregoing writing we have tried "many times and in many ways" to praise love. As we thank God that we have been able to complete the writing in the way we wished, we would now conclude by introducing John the Apostle, saying: "Beloved, let us love one another." These words, which have apostolic authority, also have, if you will consider them, a middle tone or a middle mood compared to the contrasts in love itself, which is to be explained by the fact that they are said by one who was perfected in love. You do not hear in these words the rigorousness of duty; the apostle does not say, "You *should* love one another;" but neither do you hear the intensity of inclination, or poet-passion. There is something transfigured and blessed in these words, but also a sadness which has moved over life and is tempered by the eternal. It is as if the apostle said, "Good heavens, what is all this which would hinder you from loving; what is all this which you can win by self-love? The commandment is that you *shall* love, but if you will understand yourself and life, then there would be no need to be commanded; because to love human beings is the only thing worth living for; without this love you really do not live; to love human beings is also the only blessed consolation for both time and eternity; and to love human beings is the only true sign that you are a Christian."[23]

Clearly the nature of love, as Kierkegaard describes it in *Works of Love*, is radically different from that encountered in the first volume of *Either/Or*. The concluding chapter of *Either/Or*, vol. 1, "The Seducer's Diary," gives the most extreme expression of the aesthete's view of love. Love is, in the highest degree, *interesting*: it captivates the lover, so that "A" can say of the seducer that "it was possible for him to appear as the one seduced."[24] Love is an intoxicating experience of erotic passion, in which the conquest is what is interesting, and it is interesting in the degree that it is conducted with aesthetic subtlety and artistry. As he begins the long and exquisite seduction of the young girl, whose name he does not even know, Johannes (the seducer) remarks, "I am submerged in love, ducked, as swimmers say; no wonder I am a little dazed. So much the better, so much the more I promise myself from this affair."[25] And again,

> How beautiful it is to be in love, how interesting to know that one
> is in love . . . And should I not be content, I who regard myself as
> a favorite of the gods, I who had the rare good fortune to fall in love
> again? That is something that no art, no study can elicit; it is a gift.[26]

Notice that something like the concept of grace is introduced here
by Johannes the Seducer, yet the word "gift" would more accurately be rendered by "good fortune," for no giver is assumed, no
providence, no responsibility to the person loved but only an aesthetical "responsibility" to maximize the passion in the experience. Johannes tricks Cordelia, deceives her, inflames her passion
by subtle manipulation—all for the sake of an interesting conquest. But he must keep her at a distance: "she must owe me nothing, for she must be free; love exists only in freedom,"[27] by which
he means that love exists only in the absence of any personal commitment or obligation. Love exists, as it were, for the benefit of
the lover, not the beloved.[28] It is the experience of being in love
that is interesting and, for that, an interesting person is required;
but in a real sense the person one is in love with is not loved at
all. In the case of Johannes and Cordelia, she provides the occasion
for an interesting and passionate experience for him.

> I am an aesthete, an eroticist, one who has understood the nature
> and meaning of love, who believes in love and knows it from the
> ground up, and only reserve to myself the private opinion that every
> love affair lasts at most a half year and that every relationship is
> done with as soon as one has enjoyed the climax. I know all this; I
> know, too, that the highest enjoyment one can imagine is to be
> loved—loved higher than anything in the world. To poetize oneself
> into a young woman is an art, to poetize oneself out of her, is a mas-
> terpiece, though the last depends essentially upon the first.[29]

This passage reveals the self-centered character of Johannes' love.
To be loved is higher than to love; the concept of neighbor love
is totally absent. An erotic relationship is to be enjoyed but not
maintained. It is to be enjoyed for itself, and when it is over, the
girl is to be got rid of—but in an aesthetic fashion. In the seduction of Cordelia, the entire affair is carried out with total fidel-
ity to the aesthetical requirements. The final entry of the diary reveals with shocking clarity the dehumanizing character of the
experience.

57

Why can such a night not be longer? If Alectryon could forget himself, why cannot the sun be equally sympathetic? Still it is over now, and I wish never to see her again. When a young woman has given away everything, then she is weak, then she has lost everything. Innocence in a man is a negative element; in a woman it is the substance of her being. Now all resistance is impossible, and only as long as that is present is it beautiful to love; when it has ceased, there is only weakness and habit. I do not wish to be reminded of my relation to her; she has lost her fragrance, and the time is past when a young woman is changed by her pain over her faithless lover into a heliotrope. I will have no farewell with her; nothing is more disgusting to me than a woman's tears and a woman's prayers, which alter everything and yet really mean nothing. I have loved her, but from now on, she can no longer engross my soul.[30]

While Johannes' view of love is aesthetically so extreme that it is demonic, aesthetical love in general is essentially devoid of any commitment to the person loved; in a real sense, the beloved is not loved at all but is the useful occasion for the experience of erotic passion. And this (not necessarily) in a vulgar sense. The seduction of Cordelia is carried out with aesthetic sensitivity and delicacy. But love that does not acknowledge the reality of the beloved as person, as neighbor, love that is devoid of any ethical element is, in the last analysis, lust.

It is this view of love against which Judge William argues in his first letter to "A," treating at length of what he calls the aesthetical validity of marriage. Recognizing that the experience of falling in love is natural and attractive, the judge joins the argument at this point: cannot that experience, the experience of "the first love," with its captivating beauty and deep intensity, be maintained? Is there not the possibility of its repetition in the lives of the two who are in love?[31] Must the experience of love, of falling in love, necessarily end in revulsion, or can it be repeated? If the validity of love is solely its effect on the lover, entailing no permanent bond between the lover and his beloved, then there can be no repetition, no permanence in the relationship, no marriage. Judge William argues that the marriage relationship, expressed in the marriage vows that are spoken before God, makes possible a repetition of the first love. In marriage the despair of the aesthete is thus overcome.

The judge recognizes, however, that the aesthete has provisionally persuasive arguments against marriage. "What can one rely on? Everything can change. Perhaps this being, whom now I almost worship, will change; perhaps fate may subsequently bring me into association with another being who, in truth, will be the ideal I have dreamt of."[33] In the judge's view, aesthetics clearly has no defense against such contingencies, for in the world of the aesthete there is no permanence, only the shifting sands of experiences which either interest or bore. His epistolary task is "to show that romantic love can be united with and can persist in marriage, yea, that marriage is the true transfiguration of romantic love."[33]

This transfiguration comes about by referring the first love to God; the lovers thank God for it. "With this an ennobling transformation is effected. The weakness to which the male is most prone is to imagine that he made a conquest of the girl he loves. . . . In thanking God, however, he humbles himself under his love; and truly it is far more beautiful to receive the beloved as a gift from God's hand than to have subdued the whole world in order to make a conquest of her."[34] "Now when the lovers refer their love to God, this act of thanksgiving imparts to it an absolute stamp of eternity."[35] Thus, marriage is the fulfillment of romantic love by giving it permanence. In this way the judge argues for the aesthetical validity of marriage, thereby saving aesthetics by means of the ethical.

"A," however, had argued in an immensely amusing chapter, entitled "The Rotation Method," that marriage and love are incompatible.

One must never enter into *marriage*. Husband and wife promise to love one another for eternity. That's easy enough to do but doesn't have much meaning; for if their love comes to an end in time, it will surely be ended in eternity. If, therefore, instead of saying "forever," the parties would say "until Easter," or "until the next Mayday," there would be some meaning in what they say; for then they would have said something definite, and also something that they might be able to keep. And how does marriage usually work out? After a short time one party begins to perceive that there is something wrong, then the other party complains, and cries to heaven: infidelity! infidelity! A little later the second party reaches the same standpoint, and a neutrality is established as the mutual faithlessness is waived for common contentment and pleasure. In the meantime it is too late, for there are great difficulties connected with divorce. . . . When two persons fall in love with one another and suspect that they were made for each other, it is time to have the courage to break it off; for by going on they have everything to lose and nothing to gain.[36]

Against such a cynical view the good judge strives valiantly, armed with the conviction that "just as for God nothing is impossible, so too for the religious individual nothing is impossible."[37] All love, he argues, has the characteristics of eternity, but what gives marriage its power to give permanence to the first love, is the marriage commitment—the recognition of the ethical bond between husband and wife, a bond of openness and honesty.

> "Candor, openheartedness, revelation,[38] understanding—these constitute the life principle of marriage, without which it fails to be beautiful or even moral; for that which love unites is then separated: the sensuous and the spiritual."[39]

It is the openness of the marriage relationship, the absence of secrets, the knowledge of each other that comes with honesty and understanding, that cements the relationship and keeps alive the first love. For "A," on the contrary, love succeeds only where there is mystery and secretiveness.

Constituted by honesty, openness, and trust, marriage, in Judge William's view, endures. Not even little extra-marital amorous affairs are to be feared; on the contrary they serve to nourish the divine and healthy vigor of conjugal love. "The married man who has the courage to confide in his wife that he loves another is saved by that, and the same holds true of the wife."[40] It is clear that the judge is a moral man who is innocent of any knowledge of sin as well as of the commandment against adultery. His confidence in the integrity of a moral man is unbounded. As was indicated in chapter 1, Judge William's version of the ethical man sets him up as one like unto God, knowing good and evil. Although the judge believes that marriage rightfully takes place in the church and before God, the emphasis is upon the act of commitment rather than upon divine grace; and it is the commitment that is presumed to insure the permanence of the aesthetical pleasure of the first love and of the marriage itself. Marriage is an ethical achievement with a definite aesthetical content. Although the judge speaks of it as religious, his understanding of the marriage covenant is devoid of any Christian insight or conviction.

The difference between Judge William's understanding of love and that of "A" is clear. The difference between Judge William's view of love and that of Kierkegaard in *Works of Love* is less obvious but of crucial importance. For all of his talk about the eternal in love, the judge writes only about preferential love. His problem is to show that preferential love in the form of "the first love" can, through marriage, be endlessly repeated and so achieve permanence and fulfillment. Marriage is a commitment made by husband and wife in the interests of giving permanence to their romantic love. There is no "Thou shalt," because the commandment is irrelevant where interest dictates the moral act. And there is no need for the commandment because, in the world of Judge William, there is no sin. He is a good man, proposing a reasonable and ethical course of action for good people, which will be to their advantage. Married love is portrayed by the judge in all its bourgeois, philistine comfortableness. While it is certainly an alternative to the version of aesthetical love portrayed by "A," in the last analysis both views are aesthetical: both appeal to the self-interest of those concerned. Neighbor love has no place in either.

It is worth recalling, in conclusion, that Kierkegaard regarded *Either/Or* as an aesthetical work—both volumes. The aesthetical and the ethical are equally removed from the religious—i.e., from real existence. This is a point that needs to be underscored. That can best be done by turning to a consideration of *The Sickness unto Death*.

CHAPTER FIVE

It is characteristic of Kierkegaard's authorship that he concerned himself with certain basic categories, which are found throughout his pseudonymous writings as well as in those whose authorship he claimed. Although in each such case the word is the same, its meaning varies according to the point of view of the writer. *Despair* is one such category, and it is treated by Kierkegaard in a profoundly significant way in *The Sickness unto Death*. His understanding of despair, as it is there set forth, is the subject of this chapter; but it will be helpful, first, to contrast it with Judge William's view of despair, found in the second volume of *Either/Or*.

That volume comprises two long letters from the judge, written to his young friend "A," in which the judge attempts to prevail upon "A" to give up his debilitating aestheticism and to live ethically. In the second letter the judge exhorts "A" to break out of his present cynical and pointless existence by *choosing*. Though lengthy and earnest, the judge's arguments could hardly have been persuasive. Choice for "A" is without meaning; his either/or has this familiar form: if you marry, you will regret it; if you do not marry, you will also regret it. "Do it/or don't do it—you will regret both."[1]

Apparently unable to accept the fact that "A's" existence is fundamentally amoral, the judge urges him "to choose good and evil." The decisive thing, Judge William argues, is to choose, to decide.

My either/or does not in the first instance denote the choice between good and evil; it denotes the choice whereby one chooses good *and* evil/or excludes them. Here the question is, under what determinants one would view the whole of existence and would himself live.[2]

To choose the ethical is to choose the standpoint from which the distinction between good and evil is posited. It is not a matter of choosing the good but of choosing to decide on the basis of good versus evil. The judge concedes that the aesthetical is not evil; it is, rather, neutral. Its determinants are the interesting/or the boring. To choose good and evil "is . . . not so much a question of choosing between willing the good *or* the evil, as of choosing to will, but herewith again the good and the evil are posited."[3] By the act of choosing, which is an act of will, one assumes (posits) that the alternatives are significant rather than merely arbitrary, that one alternative really is good, the other not good. A distinction between good and evil is thereby posited. In contrast to this, it matters not to "A" whether one marries or does not marry: if you marry, you will regret it; if you do not marry, you will also regret that. Where the interesting holds sway, nothing normative is presupposed or posited. If, however, instead of merely wishing, a person wills, if instead of merely letting things happen, a person chooses (decides), then there is the implicit assumption that the difference between the alternatives is not arbitrary but absolute. This is the crucial difference between the aesthetical and the ethical either/or.

In the judge's view, choice—the hallmark of the ethical—gives to life dignity and depth of meaning. "The act of choosing imparts to a man's nature a solemnity, a quiet dignity, which is never entirely lost."[4] Indeed, choosing good and evil enables a person to become himself. This the judge regards as the true goal of any person's life, "for the great thing is not to be this or that but to be oneself, *and this every one can be if he wills it*"[5] [emphasis mine]. Clearly, the ethical does not entail the notion of sin.

The judge's analysis leads him to the conclusion that the aesthetical life is despair, "and every one who lives aesthetically is in despair, whether he knows it or not,"[6] for the aesthete fails to make the decisive choice and thus fails to become himself. To live aesthetically is to live in the arbitrary and ephemeral. However enticing the young girl, however delicious the dinner, however interesting the book or the play, they flow into one's existence accidentally and, in time, they can and do become boring and their significance vanishes. Only in the ethical, the judge maintains, does existence have that permanence of structure that gives to everything its quantum of meaning. When one lives aesthetically, one lives without meaning and so is in despair. "But when one knows it," continues the judge, "(and you indeed know it), a higher form of existence is a demand that is not to be refused."[7]

This, however, is precisely what "A" does *not* know. From his perspective, the judge is fooling himself. To posit good and evil is to engage in a perhaps pleasurable delusion, but it is no more than that. The positing of good and evil is as arbitrary as the sin of Eve and Adam. It has consequences, but they are like the consequences of any other interest, no more durable or real. In "A's" view, the judge is simply positing a higher interest, and the positing of good and evil is merely an instance of wishful thinking. There is not the slightest chance that "A" will be convinced by the judge's letter, inasmuch as these two move in different worlds; they interpret existence on the basis of totally different and irreconcilable presuppositions.

After a great many pages of analysis and exhortation, Judge William tries a new tack: "What then must you do?" It is clear that "A" would feel no need to do anything that did not happen to interest him, but this obvious fact escapes the judge, who then gives his own reply: "I have only one answer: despair!"[8] Since "A's" existence, as the judge sees it, is despair, his only hope is to choose it, i.e., to acknowledge and accept his despair *as despair*, for in acknowledging to himself that he is in despair he would *ipso facto* have chosen the ethical perspective and moved beyond despair.

> So then choose despair, for despair is itself a choice; one can doubt without choosing to, but one cannot despair without choosing to.[9] And when a man despairs, he again chooses—and what is it he then chooses? He chooses himself, not in his [aesthetical] immediacy, not as this fortuitous individual, but he chooses himself in his eternal validity.[10]

Here we have the kernel of the ethical "stage." Choice rescues one from the arbitrariness of aesthetical preference, which has no staying power. It does so by positing through the act of choice the eternal distinction between good and evil. In positing that distinction, one chooses oneself in one's eternal validity; one becomes (as we have seen in the second chapter[11]) the absolute. To choose despair, to acknowledge thereby that one is in despair, frees one from it. Moreover, by choosing oneself, one chooses oneself as absolute (or, in other words, one chooses oneself in one's eternal validity). Choosing despair and choosing good and evil are the same choice, for the aesthete's despair (in the judge's view) is the amoral character of his existence, his total lack of any ethical concern. It is an impoverishment of will. Despair refers not to any feeling but to his state of being, in which the absence of the ethical constitutes a fatal deprivation.

The judge sums the matter up as follows:

> One cannot despair at all without willing it, but to despair truly one must truly will it, but when one truly wills it, *one is truly beyond despair* [emphasis mine]; when one has truly chosen despair, one has truly chosen that which despair chooses, i.e., oneself in one's eternal validity. . . .
>
> But I return to my category. I am no logician. I have only one category, but I assure you that it is both my heart's and my thought's choice, my soul's joy and my blessedness—I turn back to the significance of choosing. When I then choose absolutely, I choose despair; and in despair I choose the absolute, for I myself am the absolute; I posit the absolute, and I myself am the absolute; but in complete identity with this I may say that I choose the absolute, which chooses me, that I posit the absolute, which posits me. . . .[12]

In Judge William's view, the solution to despair is to choose it and thereby to choose the ethical—an act of will which, in his view, does not participate in the despair which it allegedly overcomes. When an individual has truly willed despair, he is beyond it. One would suppose that, if the aesthete is in despair, then any choice he might make to escape despair would be a despairing choice that would participate in the despair it seeks to escape. The judge, however, is confident that if "A" were to choose despair, his choice would be untouched by the despair that he chose and by the despair from which he sought escape.

Kierkegaard did not share this optimism. In his view human existence *is* despair. The judge, therefore, is not wrong in describing "A's" existence as despair. However, he does not recognize that his own ethical existence is also despair, for he does not recognize the despair that informs his presumption: "In despair I choose the absolute, for I myself am the absolute, I posit the absolute and I myself am the absolute. . . ."[13] This point has already been noted in the first chapter,[14] but it can be briefly summarized here. Judge William's belief that, through his own choice, he creates the distinction between good and evil, thereby according them and himself an absolute status, amounts to no more than the absolutizing of his own preferences. In the last analysis he, too, is an aesthete, although he does not recognize it ("A's" vision is clearer). To make absolute claims for one's own choices is no less arbitrary than rejecting all claims except one's desires and interests. As Kierkegaard saw it, both the aesthete and the ethicist are prototypes of despair. We turn now to his own view of despair as this is expounded in *The Sickness unto Death*.

The author of *The Sickness unto Death* is Anti-Climacus. Unlike Johannes Climacus, he is not *interested* in Christianity; he *is* a Christian. His perspective, therefore, has nothing of the experimental and hypothetical approach to fundamental existential concerns, which characterized the thought of Johannes Climacus. Anti-Climacus is clearly not typical of the pseudonyms represented by the aesthetical writings. It is tempting to identify him with Kierkegaard, but here one must be careful. Kierkegaard wrote in his journal that he was below Anti-Climacus but above Johannes Climacus, suggesting that he found himself in a tension between the experimental attitude of Climacus and the confidence of Anti-Climacus, who "supposed himself to be Christian to an extraordinary degree."[15] On balance, it is probably accurate to speak of the author of *The Sickness unto Death* as Kierkegaard, for while Kierkegaard recognized that his own faith was not the pure Christianity described in the book, and a decent humility restrained him consequently from ascribing authorship to himself, the content does indeed express his deepest Christian convictions.[16]

For Anti-Climacus despair lies in the will. The despairing man is one who does not will to be himself and, consequently, wills to be a self that he is not. For example, a man who neglects his son demonstrates thereby that he is unwilling to be his son's father. Biologically and legally, of course, the boy is his son; but in neglecting his son, the father is willing (wills) to be someone he is not—a man who refuses to take full parental responsibility for the boy's life. He *is* the boy's father, yet he is unwilling to be that; he *wills* not to be his son's father. Thus, he is in fact unwilling to be himself, and what is the same, he wills (despairingly) to be a self he is not: a man without the burden of this son.

Let us look at this view of despair in greater detail. Anti-Climacus begins his analysis with a somewhat cryptic description of the self, starting with the assertion that a human being is spirit, and spirit is the self.[17] From what follows, it is clear that "spirit" refers to man's[18] self-transcendence, to the fact that he stands always beyond himself and cannot therefore escape from deciding what he is and what he must do to become himself. Anti-Climacus expresses this by saying that the self is a relation that relates itself to itself. Man (as such) is a relation between two factors, the infinite and the finite, the temporal and the eternal, possibility and necessity.[19] From the last description, it is clear that man is a relation (Anti-Climacus also uses the term synthesis) of past and future. Our past is absolutely and irrevocably what it is; fixed and unchangeable, it is our necessity. Our future, on the other hand, is possibility—not, to be sure, unlimited possibility, but all the possibilities that are relevant to our own past, if only the possibility of pretending that our past is other than it is and so of attempting to become someone we are not.

But, the self as a synthesis of necessity and possibility describes man in general. I am not, however, just *a* self, a particular instance of human being. I am (and this is of inescapable concern to me) *my*self, a fact that constitutes a task, namely the task to become *me*.[20] No one can live *my* life for me, make my decisions for me, think my thoughts for me, discharge my responsibilities for me, do my dying for me, although we constantly try to get some person or other to do just that, thus displaying that form of despair which Anti-Climacus characterizes as being unwilling to be oneself.

Now Anti-Climacus moves one step further. "Such a relation which relates itself to itself (that is to say, a self) must either have established itself or have been established by another." Without argument he assumes that it has been constituted by another, and he concludes, "Such a derived, constituted, relation is the human self, a relation which relates itself to its self, and in relating itself to itself relates itself to another." It is an established, or constituted, self-relation, i.e., it is a relation that is posited not by the self, but by a Power beyond the self, which Anti-Climacus subsequently identifies as God. In contrast to the position of Judge William, who posits himself absolutely, chooses himself in his eternal validity, Anti-Climacus asserts that the self is posited by another.

In this section of the book we have only bare assertion, unbuttressed by argument. The absence of argument indicates that it is a confessional statement. Anti-Climacus does not argue for the nature of the self, because it is not a philosophical anthropology that is here being delineated but, rather, a Christian doctrine of man. Christianity is not something that is reached at the end of a chain of reasoning; it is a faith that can be expressed *through* reason but not attained or justified *by* it. *The Sickness unto Death* is a Christian work, a confession of faith; its presuppositions, concisely articulated in its first pages, are likewise confessional in nature. Unlike Johannes Climacus, whose chain of reasoning moves from a hypothesis experimentally adopted out of idle interest, Anti-Climacus simply states in rational form the faith from which his reflection moves. In somewhat unusual, certainly non-traditional, language he expresses the traditional Christian belief that God created man in his own image.

Man, then, is a relation, a synthesis of finite and infinite, necessity and possibility. A *self* is a relation that relates itself to itself and in relating itself to itself relates itself to another. To become myself, I must relate myself to the relation that is my humanity; I must will to accept responsibility for my own living, my own deciding, and so for my own past and my own future in their union, which is my present. This in turn means that I must accept the necessity that defines me: my body and my mind, with their strengths and weaknesses, my spouse, my children, all past decisions, by which I am inescapably bound, be they made wisely or witlessly, and so on. Further, all my decisions must be made with reference to the possibilities that constitute *my* future and not another's. Decision, moreover, is something that I cannot avoid, for not to decide is always to have decided. Decide I must; this is an inescapable imperative of human life. In short, to be myself means that I must will to be the person I, in fact, am—to accept the responsibilities that constitute me as this particular historical being, quite apart from whether or not I like me. Despair is the unwillingness to do this.

Therefore, there are in Anti-Climacus' view two forms of despair, although in the last analysis despair is one thing. The forms are, first, not to will to be oneself, and second, *despairingly* to will to be oneself, i.e., to will to be a self one is not. Had the self established itself, there would be but one form: being unwilling to be oneself, i.e., simply refusing, in Judge William's terms, to choose oneself in one's eternal validity. Despair would be a failure of nerve, the unwillingness to accept responsibility for one's ideas and actions. Such is the life of the aesthete. A classic form of the unwillingness to be oneself is the practice of suicide, which was commended by the ancient Stoics. When appropriate or convenient, a person simply bowed out of life, unwilling any longer to accept its burdens and pain, yet doing so without defiance, since for the Stoics there was no Power who set to each individual the task that he alone could and should fulfill: that of being *him*self. The doctrine of vocation separates Stoicism and Christianity decisively.

Where, however, the relation in relating itself to itself is related to Another who has constituted it, then there is another form of despair, defiance: willing *despairingly* to be oneself, i.e., refusing to be the self that the Power has constituted and so willing positively, defiantly, to be a self that one is not. It is crucially important to recognize that the verb *will* is used here, not in the sense of simply being in agreement (for example, "I am willing to do this for you, since you ask me to") but in the active and positive sense that the self wills not to be itself—or despairingly, defiantly, wills to be a self it is not, refusing to be the person God wills it to be. Out of resentment one hates God and defiantly rebels against being who one essentially is.

Given this view of despair, it is clear that one cannot will oneself out of despair, because the will to be free of despair is a despairing will. St. Augustine's well-known prayer comes to mind: Lord grant me chastity and continence—but not yet. "If the despairing person is aware of his despair, . . ." writes Anti-Climacus, "and does not speak meaninglessly of it as of something that is happening to him . . . and now with all his power seeks to break the despair by himself and by himself alone—he is still in despair and with all his presumed effort only works himself all the deeper into deeper despair." Judge William claims that if one truly wills despair, one is *ipso facto* beyond it; Anti-Climacus asserts that any attempt to escape despair is a despairing attempt and so mires the despairer more deeply in his despair. Despair is the state of actively willing not to be oneself or willing to be a self one is not—which comes to the same thing. The despairer wills unceasingly to despair; it is his state of being, that persists through time; hence, "choosing despair" is meaningless, because such "freedom of choice" is not an existential possibility. In despair, the individual rejects both his true self and the Power that has constituted him, and his will is in contradiction with itself.

The opposite of despair, then, would be to will to be oneself.

"This, then, is the formula which describes the condition of the self when despair is completely rooted out: by relating itself to its own self and by willing to be itself the self is grounded transparently in the Power which posited it."

But how does this happen? How is despair completely eradicated? According to Judge William, "the great thing is not to be this or that but to be oneself, and this everyone can be if he wills it."[21] In contrast, Anti-Climacus underscores the impossibility of willing oneself out of despair, because a despairing will can only will itself deeper into despair. There is but one possibility by which despair can be eradicated—the Possibility that is God, for whom all things are possible. "But the critical decision does not come until a person is brought to the extreme, when humanly speaking there is no possibility. Then the question is whether he will believe that for God everything is possible, that is, whether he will *believe*." A few lines farther on, in a strikingly beautiful passage, Anti-Climacus writes,

> So then, salvation is humanly speaking the most impossible thing of all; but for God all things are possible! This is the fight of *faith*, which fights madly (if one would so express it) for possibility, for possibility is the only salvation. . . . And so the fight goes on. Whether he who is engaged in this fight will be defeated depends solely and alone upon whether he has the will to procure possibility, that is to say, whether he will believe. And yet he understands that humanly speaking his ruin is the most certain thing of all. . . .[22] To *believe* in his own ruin is impossible. To understand that humanly speaking it is his ruin and then nevertheless to believe in possibility, is to believe. Then God helps him—perhaps by letting him escape the horror, perhaps through the horror itself—in that here, unexpectedly, miraculously, divinely, help appears. . . . Whether a man has been helped by a miracle depends essentially upon the degree of intellectual passion he has employed to understand that help was impossible, and next upon how honest he is toward the Power which helped him nevertheless."[23]

Despair, then, is a sickness of the will; and it is a "sickness unto death," because it is an actively, continually willed self-denial or self-negation, a dying that does not terminate in death's release but condemns the despairer to dying the death, i.e., to negating himself in every act of affirming himself. He wills to

70

live a contradiction, from which he cannot escape, *because he will not.*

But what about suicide, one might ask? Is not this a way out? Suicide may well result in being rid of the *consciousness* of despair but not its reality, for by committing suicide one does not, thereby, will to be oneself nor, manifestly, does one become oneself. For example, a mother whose weakness or neurotic personality has become the occasion for her child's defeat in life is in despair at not willing to be herself—at not willing to be that child's mother, or what is the same, at willing to deny herself through abdicating her responsibilities. That her neglect was compulsive, in a sense involuntary, does not alter the objective situation. By eliminating herself, she will neither make redress nor heal herself of her infidelity (nor, incidentally, of her neurosis). She will carry her despair with her into the grave and heap still more misery and guilt on the child, over whose suffering she had deceived herself into supposing that she had despaired. She was, in fact, in despair over herself, that she was unwilling to be herself, to be her child's mother, but instead willed to be a self that took the easy way out.

In subsequent chapters, Anti-Climacus delineates the forms which despair takes, first by considering them abstractly in terms of the synthesis that is man. Thus there is the despair of finitude due to lack of infinitude, of infinitude due to lack of finitude, and so on. He then continues by considering the gradations of despair according to the degree of consciousness of despair, beginning with the most common form of despair, which is being unconscious that one is in despair, and ending with "the despair of willing despairingly to be oneself—defiance." The analysis of despair both formally and in its various manifestations constitutes Part I of *The Sickness unto Death.*

Part II is a parallel analysis of sin.

> Sin is: *before God, or with the conception [forestilling] of God, in despair not to will to be oneself, or in despair to will to be oneself.* Thus sin is intensified weakness or intensified defiance: sin is the intensification of despair. The emphasis is on *before God.*[24]

Accordingly sin is not an ethical category.

> Very often . . . it is overlooked that the opposite of sin is by no means virtue. In part, this is a pagan view, which is satisfied with a merely

human criterion and simply does not know what sin is, that all sin is before God. No, *the opposite of sin is faith. . . .*[25]

In this second half of the book, Anti-Climacus lays bare with profound insight and tremendous power the human soul in its existential dilemma. I will mention only one of these insights: his treatment of *offense*. That God should be concerned with the sin of any individual is an offense to that person, for it implies that God's love reaches out to every individual: "Not a sparrow falls. . . ." In a world where speculative thought holds sway, the individual is offended by this—offended because he cannot find any convincing way to think it, yet he so greatly desires it.

> [Offense] lies in this, that a human being should have this reality [Realitet]: that as an *individual* human being a person is directly before God and consequently, as a corollary, that a person's sin should be of concern to God. The idea of the individual human being—before God— speculation never gets into its head. It only universalizes individual human beings fantastically into the race. . . . There is so much talk about being offended by Christianity because it is so dark and gloomy, offended because it is so rigorous etc., but it would be best of all to explain for once that the real reason that men are offended by Christianity is that it is too high, because its goal is not man's goal, because it wants to make man into something so extraordinary that he can't get it into his head.[26]

The sinner cannot tolerate the love of God for *him*. He desires it above all else; he is offended by it totally. Anti-Climacus emphasizes the incommensurability between what reason tells us is possible and what every person deeply desires (in Pascal's phrase, what is the reason of the heart), namely, to matter ultimately, to count as an individual in this vast universe, to be remembered ultimately, to believe that God does love him or her. The obvious rational inference from considering our insignificant place in a boundless universe is that we are but drops of water in life's vast ocean, that God may well be concerned with humanity as such, with justice among the nations or the galaxies. But, that God is concerned about the individual, about *me*—that strains credulity, it is preposterous and, above all, it offends—because everyone deeply wants to believe it. It is painful in the extreme to bear the reality of human loneliness, but cosmic loneliness we seldom feel, because its pain is too great to acknowledge.

Sin is, before God, to be in despair. Sin is to take offense at the love of God. These are the same, and they mean that one is unwilling to be who one is: a creature of God, loved by God, saved by Christ.

It is clear that there is no kinship between the Christian faith of Anti-Climacus on the one hand, and the atheism of both "A" and Judge William on the other. To be sure, "A's" atheism is more subtle than the judge's—and more honest. For "A," God is so irrelevant as to be unreal. The judge, in contrast, speaks often of God, approves of the church and of its role in marriage. But in the last analysis, the ethical man is autonomous: he posits good and evil, posits himself as absolute, and is, to all intents and purposes, God in his own right.[27] Anti-Climacus expresses the Christian faith in so pure a form that Kierkegaard felt the need to write *The Sickness unto Death* under a pseudonym. The book expressed, however, the faith he longed for and to whose proclamation his life, like his authorship, was deeply committed.

CHAPTER SIX

Perhaps the best way to conclude this brief study of Kierkegaard's pseudonymous writings is to question its basic premise, which is that Kierkegaard's own interpretation of his authorship, given in *The Point of View*, is correct. In that book Kierkegaard explains that the pseudonymous works (except those by Anti-Climacus) were intended as an ironic and subtle assault on what he regarded as the delusive Christianity of Copenhagen's Christians. It was an attack upon the "monstrous illusion" that obtained in that Christian land, where all were Christians by virtue of having been born Danes. By inveigling the unsuspecting reader into identifying with an ironic statement of his own perspective, with the intention that the reader would become aware of its actual significance for his life as well as its radical difference from Christian belief, Kierkegaard hoped to compel at least a few to take notice and then to judge for themselves. This is the clear account of the authorship that is given in *The Point of View*. There are, however, arguments that can be advanced against its acceptance, and these we should now consider.

For one thing, we know that Kierkegaard began his passionate, almost compulsive career as an author immediately after the break with Regine Olsen. The profound grief and guilt that he experienced in those first months and years clearly informed his early writing. In addition, he was deeply concerned to clarify the reasons for his action and to justify what he had done. *Fear and Trembling*, for example, was implicitly addressed to Regine, wrestling, as it does, with the problem of transcending ethical duty for a "higher duty"—precisely Kierkegaard's problem in breaking the engagement. Ethically, he was bound by his commitment to Regine; he had confessed his love to her, asked for her hand, and pledged his word. Ethically, his duty was clear: to keep his word to her. But in his inmost being, the silent knowledge of the impossibility of marriage required him to break his word and to pursue a course of action that ethically was without justification.

His dilemma is also set forth in *Either/Or*, in which he explored the alternatives of a complacent pursuit of the interesting and the pleasurable on the one hand, and a stern adherence to duty on the other. Thus, "The Seducer's Diary" presents the picture of a sophisticated and heartless scoundrel, who would manipulate a young woman into falling in love with him, only to abandon her when he had succeeded. This is contrasted with the romantic yet sober view of marriage and home described by Judge William in the second volume. Kierkegaard doubtless hoped that Regine would read with recognition and then decide which picture he most closely resembled.

As a result of his unhappy love for Regine, Kierkegaard became a poet, living largely through a passionate devotion to the idea (for example, of love) rather than the reality. A poet-existence [*en Digter-Existents*] is characterized by alienation, and so by deprivation and consequent suffering. Later in his life—in *The Sickness unto Death*—he says of a poet-existence, "Christianly understood, every poet-existence . . . is sin, the sin of poetizing instead of being, of relating to the good and the true through imagination[1] instead of being that—that is, existentially striving to be that.[2]"

In his journal of 1843 he says of *Either/Or*, "The first diapsalma[3] is really the work's entire task, which finds its solution only in the preacher's last word."[4] Here is part of the first diapsalma:

> What is a poet? A poet is an unhappy being, who hides deep torments in his heart, but whose lips are so formed that as the sighs and the cries escape them, they sound like beautiful music. His fate is like those unfortunates who in the brazen bull of Phalaris were slowly tortured over a steady fire; their cries could not reach the tyrant's ears so as to strike terror into his heart; to him they sounded like sweet music. And people flock around the poet and say to him,

"Sing again soon!" which is to say, "May new sufferings torture your soul."[5]

That Kierkegaard was speaking of his own life is obvious.

The second volume of *Either/Or* ends with a sermon by an unnamed Jutland priest, in tone quite different both from "A's" aestheticism and Judge William's moralism. The sermon concludes with the words, "Only the truth that uplifts[6] is truth for you." Kierkegaard's life as a poet—and this was most of his life—was one of suffering, but he sought and ultimately found the truth that uplifts; it was this truth that he set forth in his religious works, published under his own name.

But, prior to becoming secure in faith, Kierkegaard experienced the tension between the aesthetical and the ethical, which is the basic substance of *Either/Or* and is especially descriptive of Kierkegaard's early life. The stern moralism of his father had not been lost on him; his aesthetical impulses were challenged by his conscience—probably a harsh superego. On the other hand, Kierkegaard was well acquainted from his student days with the aesthetical life. He was possessed of undoubted charm and wit and cleverness, and he knew his own potential for casting a captivating spell on a young woman like Regine. As yet, he was not a man of faith. "Had I had faith, I would have remained with Regine," he wrote in his journal in May of 1843. "Praise and thanks to God that I now see this. I have come close to losing my mind in recent days."[7] Indeed, the situation in which any person lacking faith finds himself is precisely that delineated by *Either/Or:* suspended, or rather swinging, between the two extremes of the aesthetical and the ethical. Theologically speaking, sin drives a wedge deep into human existence, so that the "I want" and the "I ought," both inescapable components of human existence, are in constant opposition. If he had had faith, he might have married Regine; as it was, he was torturously torn by the conflict between what he most wanted in life and what he knew to be his duty. This same journal entry, quoted above, continues:

> Humanly speaking I did right toward her. Perhaps I ought never to have become engaged, but from that moment I acted honorably toward her. In aesthetic and knightly terms I loved her far more than she loved me; for otherwise she would never have evinced pride to-

ward me or later on caused me anxiety with her cries. I have started on a story entitled "Guilty/not Guilty."[8] Naturally it will contain things that will surprise the world; for in a year and a half I have lived through more of the poetic than all novels put together. But I cannot and will not let my relationship to her be poetically weakened; it has an entirely other reality. She has not become some theatrical princess; if possible she shall become my wife. Dear God, that was my only desire, and yet I had to deny myself that. And in this I was, humanly speaking, completely right and have acted with a high degree of nobility toward her by not letting her suspect my pain. In purely aesthetical terms I have been a decent person (I dare give myself that much praise), and I have done what few in my position would have done; for had I not thought so much about her welfare, I could have had her (she herself begged for that—which she certainly never should have done; it was a deceitful weapon) . . . God is my witness that it was my only desire; God is my witness, how I have watched over myself, that no forgetfulness should erase my memory of her; I have not spoken, I believe, to any young woman since that time. . . .[9]

His suffering was the nearly unbearable tension he experienced between his desire and his duty—between the aesthetical and the ethical.

When he wrote *Either/Or*, Kierkegaard clearly had in mind his experience with Regine. Like any author, he necessarily wrote out of his own experience; but Kierkegaard made certain that his personal history did not intrude into his writing, even though, in a profound sense, it provided its substance. Regine could read in the book what others would not see, and he left her free to decide whether or not he was the cad he had pretended to be. She had made him a poet; his continuing love for her and his loss of her were his inspiration. "He continued to love 'Her' to the end of his life—and she, outliving him by many years, and outliving her husband, continued to love him. He had not succeeded in making her believe he was a scoundrel."[10]

In the period when he wrote and published (1843) *Either/Or, Fear and Trembling*, and *Repetition*, the suffering occasioned by his unhappy love was certainly uppermost in his mind. But the religious motive was also present, as witnessed by the simultaneous publication of three volumes of edifying discourses and by the inclusion of the sermon with which *Either/Or* ends. Kierkegaard constantly reflected on his work as an author, struggling to clarify his motivation. In 1849, he wrote in his journal,

> Yet a last attempt I have made to say something about myself and the whole of my authorship. . . . The thing is, I see with extraordinary clarity the infinitely ingenious thought that is in the authorship's totality. . . . To take an example, it is true that when I began as an author I was "religiously resolved," but this must be understood in another way. *Either/Or*, especially "The Seducer's Diary," I wrote for her sake, in order to clear her out of the relationship. On the whole the very mark of my genius is that Governance broadens and radicalizes whatever concerns me personally.[11]

Regine was indeed central to these early writings. That he sought to explain himself to her (and to himself) did not, however, negate or exclude his religious concern. That concern was the problem of how to become a Christian in Christendom. Nor was his abiding sense of the presence of Divine Providence ever out of his mind. His work, which he recognized to be the work of genius, could only be understood and accomplished in obedience to God's will. "For I am a genius in this sense, that I cannot quite simply take personal responsibility for the whole without infringing on Governance."[12] It can be argued, of course, that hindsight is always 20/20, and that Kierkegaard can hardly have had the plan of authorship in its totality clearly in mind when he began to write *Either/Or*. Psychologically speaking, this point has a strong factor of plausibility, even probability. One might equally well argue, however, that his later interpretation has a like plausibility: that throughout his years of writing, his religious concern was unconsciously shaping the pattern of his authorship without his being quite conscious of its evolving shape.

Such arguments are necessarily speculative and inconclusive. The question persists as to whether the interpretation of the authorship found in *The Point of View* is plausible or even possible. Kierkegaard was aware of the problem, and he addressed it squarely in that book. Reflecting on the part which Governance played in the whole authorship and on his recognition of it, he writes,

> If I were to go ahead and say that from the very beginning I had had a clear view of the whole dialectical construction of the entire au-

thorship, or that at every moment, step by step, I had by anticipation
so far exhausted the possibilities that later reflection had not taught
me anything, or at times something different; that what I had done
was surely right, yet only now did I myself correctly understand it
—if I were to do this, then it would be a denial of God and dishonesty towards Him. No, I must say truly that I cannot understand the
whole, just because to the merest insignificant detail I understand
the whole; but what I cannot understand is that now I can understand it and yet by no means dare say that at the moment of com-
mencing it I understood it so precisely—and yet I am the one who
carried it out and took every step with reflection.[13]

The paradoxical character of the last sentence of this passage expresses precisely Kierkegaard's understanding of his work. He cannot understand the whole despite understanding it to the most
minute detail because, like any mortal, he cannot understand the
ways of Providence that, in his case, informed an aesthetical authorship with religious purpose. What he cannot understand—and
for the same reason—is that now he understands it completely,
although he lacked that understanding when he began his writing:
"yet I am the one who carried it out and took every step with reflection." To put it another way, he was unable to resolve the contradiction between understanding the pattern of his work, and yet
not understanding how his task and his abilities were given to him.
God's presence in his life, guiding and governing him through suffering and sublime literary achievement, was a mystery that defied
understanding.

He goes on to acknowledge that superficially the matter could
be accounted for by claiming, as some contemporaries did, that he
had a genius for reflection; but this, he asserts, reveals a misunderstanding of both categories. He can understand his work and
his life only by reference to Governance.

Were I now to express with the utmost categorical precision the part
that Governance had in my whole activity as a writer, I know of no
more suggestive or decisive expression than this: it is Governance
that has educated[14] me, and the education is reflected in the pro-
ductivity's process. In a way, what was said above becomes then in
one sense not quite true, namely that the entire aesthetical production is a deceit, for this expression concedes a little too much in the
direction of consciousness. At the same time, however, it is not al-

together false, for I have been conscious of being under [divine] tutelage [*opdragelse*] from the very first. This was the process: a poetic and philosophic nature is put aside in order to become a Christian. But the unusual feature is that *the two movements begin simultaneously* [emphasis mine], and hence this is a conscious process; one is able to see how it takes place. The second movement does not commence after a period of years that separate it from the first. So the aesthetic production is, to be sure, a deceit, yet in another sense it is a necessary evacuation [*udtommelse*, lit. emptying out]. From the very first moment the religious is decisively present, has a decisive predominance, but for a while waits patiently while the poet has leave to talk himself out. . . .[15]

Thus, the pseudonymous writings were indeed for Kierkegaard aesthetical. The point of view of *Either/Or* and *Fear and Trembling* is aesthetical and not religious (and this includes the moralizing of Judge William). The predominant conscious motivation in writing these books was doubtless Kierkegaard's need to empty out of himself the conflicting feelings about his love for and break with Regine. Although at the time he but dimly perceived it, he later recognized these works to be integral parts of a larger plan in the service of Governance. Their ironic character and polemical purpose were certainly not afterthoughts. Kierkegaard knew what he was doing when he wrote them, but he did not see clearly the overall plan of his literary activity until he had written much more.

Was Kierkegaard the author of this plan? In a sense, yes. As the pieces fell in place, his religious vocation became progressively clearer to him, and he wrote *The Point of View* to set it forth. But in another sense—in his own deeply felt Christian conviction—he was not the author but the instrument. Governance guided his entire life and, above all, his work as an author. Conscious from the very first of being under instruction, he wrote as he had to write, and was guided toward the religious goal of the total authorship. Thus the aesthetic production was in one sense a deceit, the attempt to deceive the reader into the truth. In another sense it was also not a deceit, precisely because it was in the divine plan, an expression of Governance's will for him.

It is certainly possible to have an understanding of Kierkegaard's work without reference to Providence, and such an understanding can be complete—*humanly speaking*. It can also reflect much of what Kierkegaard himself would have said of his work.

But it will not illuminate his final understanding of the matter. As far as he was concerned, it was impossible to understand his life's work without recognizing the role of Governance in it. True, he wrote the aesthetical works in large part, at least, for aesthetical reasons. He would speak to Regine. But this aesthetical purpose was subsumed under a more embracing religious purpose, the significance of which was to become clear to him only later in his life. It may properly be asked whether the canons of biographical writing admit of invoking the part which Governance plays in a person's life. In a secular age the answer is almost certainly to be in the negative. On the other hand, it must be recognized that a negative answer dictates an explanation of Kierkegaard's life work that distorts it in a fundamental way. A reductionist explanation necessarily fails to account for what, in his view, was central to his authorship. Kierkegaard was a religious author, he was a Christian and, as far as he was concerned, his work could only be understood on the basis of the role of Governance in his life and authorship.

Finally, we return to the thesis posed at the outset: that the key to understanding Kierkegaard's pseudonymous authorship is his use of irony. Why did he expend such enormous effort in writing these works, whose ironic purpose has so often and so easily escaped his readers' perception? The first answer to that question must be, as has already been noted, that Kierkegaard was himself extremely ironical. Irony came naturally to him. Yet, that irony is conspicuously missing from the later Christian works, such as *The Sickness unto Death* and *Works of Love*. The ironic character of the pseudonymous works was a necessary vehicle of their meaning and purpose, consciously embraced. In short, he had his reasons for the irony that informed his pseudonymous writing.

It will be recalled that Kierkegaard describes Christendom as "a monstrous illusion."[16] How is it possible to persuade a person who is suffering from an illusion that his beliefs are just that— illusory? As every psychotherapist will testify, this is no easy task, and it is especially difficult where religious beliefs are at issue. We protect our religious convictions compulsively; defensiveness characterizes any religious stance, because in a very real sense our life depends on it. Bluntly, if accurately, to have challenged the Christianity of his time, backed as it was by the whole authority of both church and state, would have been a futile undertaking, as well as destructive, of any influence Kierkegaard might have had. With profound psychological insight, he explained his reasons for his approach.

> That there must be here [in Christendom] a tremendous confusion, a frightful illusion, there surely can be no doubt. But to meddle with it! Yes, I know the objections well. For there are those who understand what I mean, but would say with a good-natured slap on the back, "My dear fellow, you are still rather young. . . . To start such a thing is certain ruin."[17]
>
> No, an illusion can never be destroyed directly, and only by indirect means can it be radically removed. If it is an illusion that all are Christians—and if something is to be done about it, it must be done indirectly, not by one who vociferously proclaims himself an extraordinary Christian, but by one who, better instructed, is ready to declare that he is not a Christian at all. That is, one must approach from behind the person who is under an illusion.[18]

Observing that the greater number of people in Christendom, while imagining themselves to be Christians, yet live in aesthetic or, at most, aesthetic-ethical categories, Kierkegaard continues:

> Suppose then that a religious writer right from the ground up has become aware of this illusion, Christendom, and so far as his strength permits (with God's aid, be it noted) would stamp it out—what then is he to do? First and foremost, no impatience. If he becomes impatient, he will rush headlong against it and accomplish nothing. A direct attack only strengthens a person in his illusion, and at the same time embitters him. There is nothing that requires such gentle handling as an illusion, in order to dispel it. If one causes the deluded one to set his will in opposition, all is lost.[19]

The religious writer must, therefore, first get in touch with his readers where they are. That is, he must begin with aesthetic achievement. Accordingly, Kierkegaard began with the aesthetical, not denouncing "its magical charms" but portraying it in all its allurement. "But above all," he adds, "do not forget one thing: what you have in mind: that it is the religious which you must bring forward."[20] But this cannot be brought forward directly. It is only by ironically disclosing the ultimate bankruptcy of the aesthetical, its despair, that one can insinuate the one under illusion into the truth. There is no direct way. After all, the one who is under an illusion is sure that he *is* a Christian; how can he then make sense of another's effort to convince him to *become* a Christian? The people whom the teacher would convince are already Christians, although in actuality they live their lives in aesthetic categories, unaware that these are not Christian.

> So then when a religious author in Christendom whose entire thought is the task of becoming a Christian would do all that he possibly can to make people take notice (for whether he succeeds or not is another question), he must begin as an aesthetic writer, and up to a definite point he must maintain this role. But there is necessarily a limit; for the aim of it is to make people take notice. And one thing the author must not forget, namely, which is which: that the religious is the decisive thing, the aesthetical the incognito—lest the dialectical interchange end in twaddle.[21]

The aesthetical work, then, is a deception—the deception characteristic of all irony. Its religious purpose, be it noted, is to deceive the reader into the truth—the truth that existence characterized by the aesthetical is despair.

If someone is shocked into taking notice of this truth, a crisis is thereby provoked in his life, and the possibility that he may be moved to relate to God honestly, i.e., as sinner, can be entertained. Irony is a powerful force, that can wake someone to the true meaning of his error and thereby point in the direction of the truth.

If the pervasive element of irony in the pseudonymous aesthetical works is overlooked, Kierkegaard's purpose is missed. Moreover, one is left to draw the unavoidable conclusion that he did not know his own mind, writing book after book with no consistency of perspective and with assertions that contradict each other in the most obvious way. Also, one is then tempted to regard the pseudonyms as existentially real persons rather than as abstract types, and, thereby, to make assessments of their books that are wide of the mark.

Kierkegaard's work as an author is a work of genius. It is as well a work of a man deeply troubled by guilt and melancholy and by the ineradicable hurt of an unhappy love. Most important, it is a work of religious purpose, the work of a man who sought to impart honesty to Christendom and, through his vocation as a religious author, to stand before God—in faith to will the one thing needful: to will to be himself.

APPENDIX

Kierkegaard's pseudonymous writings have been accorded a wide variety of interpretations, ranging from a simple acceptance of his statement in "A First and Last Explanation [*Forklaring*]" that not a word of the pseudonyms is his[1] to its total disregard.[2] The vast majority fall in the latter group. In this appendix we sample some of the ways in which the pseudonymous authorship has been treated.

Earlier writers on Kierkegaard, like Walter Lowrie, David F. Swenson, and Eduard Geismar, do not, so far as I am aware, deal with the ironic character of Kierkegaard's pseudonymous writings or question to what extent, if at all, these writings represent Kierkegaard's own convictions. For example, in the index to Swenson's *Something about Kierkegaard*, the word *irony* does not appear. In his Stone Lectures, *Lectures on the Religious Thought of Søren Kierkegaard*, Geismar recognizes the integrity of the pseudonymous authors and, in dealing with *Either/Or* and *Repetition*, does not identify their authors with Kierkegaard. However, in writing about the *Postscript* and the *Fragments*, he assumes that Johannes Climacus speaks for Kierkegaard. But he nowhere notes the ironic character of the pseudonymous production.

Reidar Thompte, writing in 1948 on Kierkegaard's philosophy of religion in a book by that title, recognizes the varied characters of the pseudonyms, especially those in *Either/Or* but, when he comes to the works of Johannes Climacus, he assumes that Kierkegaard is speaking in them, and he takes Climacus' distinctions between Religiousness A and Religiousness B, as well as his observations on irony and humor, as expressions of Kierkegaard's philosophy of religion. He quotes with approval Climacus' well-known assertion: "An objective uncertainty held fast in an appropriation-process of the most passionate inwardness is the truth, the highest truth attainable for an existing individual," and he believes that this expresses Kierkegaard's own view. Thompte has little to say about irony, confining himself to what Climacus has written in the *Postscript*, and nowhere suggesting its dominant role in the pseudonymous writings as a whole. In fairness, however, it must be said that Thompte's book is unusual for the period, in its recognition of the pseudonyms and its wealth of insight.

In the last couple of decades, the problem of the relationship of Kierkegaard to his pseudonyms has come to the fore, as more attention has been paid both to this "First and Last Explanation" and to his own account of the pseudonymous authorship set forth in the *Point of View*, but even many recent commentators pay the matter scant heed. For example, John W. Elrod in his book, *Being and Existence in Kierkegaard's Pseudonymous Works*, undertakes to show that, in addressing himself to the nature of the self, Kierkegaard developed in the pseudonymous works an ontology. Yet, no slightest recognition of the independent character of the pseudonyms graces these pages, nor of the ironic character of the pseudonymous books. Everything said by the pseudonyms is ascribed to Kierkegaard without qualification.

Similarly, in the Preface to his book, *The Logic of Subjectivity: Kierkegaard's Philosophy of Religion*, Louis Poyman writes, "I claim that Kierkegaard was, among other things, a philosopher, a Christian philosopher,"[3] but to make his case Poyman has recourse almost exclusively to *Philosophical Fragments* and *Concluding Unscientific Postscript*, without any regard to the significance of the pseudonymous authorship of these works. As argued above in chapter 3, Climacus is not Kierkegaard; moreover, these books were for Kierkegaard aesthetical writings and hence not Christian. Poyman even recognizes this when he asserts that the aesthetical works show that the aesthetical leads to a dead end and cannot be confused with Christianity, yet he speaks, for example, of "Kierkegaard's thought experiment,"[4] which is explicitly Climacus' and, by virtue of its skeptical presuppositions, cannot possibly be Kierkegaard's Christian view.

In 1962, Princeton University Press republished *Philosophical Fragments* in a revised translation. The edition contained an Introduction and an extensive Commentary, both written by Professor Niels Thulstrup of the University of Copenhagen, one of the foremost contemporary Kierkegaardian scholars. Thulstrup does not, however, recognize the ironic character of *Fragments* nor the fact that Johannes Climacus does not speak for Kierkegaard. He refers to Johannes as "the book's supposed author" and attributes its content, without reservation, to Kierkegaard himself. To cite an extreme example of this confusion, I refer to Thulstrup's summary of Climacus' analogy of the king who loved the humble maiden—an analogy to the god's love for mankind.[5] Writes Thulstrup:

> Such a king cannot in a direct way and in the categories of immediacy bring about the equality which is the goal; if he were to appear before the beloved, the humble maiden, in his glory and majesty, he would repel her. A solution must be found for this difficulty; the union, the understanding of the beloved, must be brought about.

After detailing the king's [the god's] difficulties, Thulstrup continues:

> The union therefore can be achieved not by an elevation . . . but by a descent, whereby God[6] appears not in his glory but in poverty, "in the form of a servant," which is his true form, not merely an outer garment. God becomes true man, does not merely seem to be a human being. Here Kierkegaard is clearly in opposition to Docetism. . . . The result is that God . . . must endure all things, must die forsaken, misunderstood by men who instead of loving him hang him on a cross.[7]

No mention is made of the fact that this is *the poet's* solution[8] as he comes to the god's help—one of the most ironic passages in *Fragments*. Thulstrup treats it as though it were serious Christian theology. Throughout his Introduction and Commentary he ascribes the views expressed in *Fragments* to Kierkegaard.

Alasdair MacIntyre's *After Virtue* is, of course, not a study of Kierkegaard, but in appealing to Kierkegaard in support of his book's main argument, he illustrates nicely the way in which Kierkegaard is so often treated—or mistreated. MacIntyre's interest is with *Either/Or*, in which he believes that he finds support for his

87

thesis. In developing his case, MacIntyre ascribes to Kierkegaard[9] the views of Judge William, especially the judge's notion of the way in which good and evil are posited through an absolute choice. He further believes that what Kierkegaard did in creating the pseudonyms was to divide up the self "and to allocate it among a series of masks, each of which acts out the masquerade of an independent self."[10] *Either/Or*'s "A" and "B" (Judge William) are alleged to be good examples of this. Thus initially MacIntyre recognizes that neither pseudonym speaks for Kierkegaard, but then surprisingly he goes on to assert, with no supporting evidence, that Judge William does so. This somewhat baffling move is found in the following passage:

> Kierkegaard . . . presents himself as not endorsing either position. For he is neither "A" nor "B." And if we take him to be presenting the position that there are no rational grounds for the choice between either position, . . .[11] he denies that too, for he is not Victor Eremita any more than he is "A" or "B." Yet at the same time he is everywhere, and perhaps we detect his presence most of all in the belief that he puts into the mouth of "B," that anyone who faces the choice between the aesthetic and the ethical will in fact choose the ethical.[12]

Thus, MacIntyre ends by asserting what he has just denied.

Admitting that his understanding of the relation of these pseudonyms to Kierkegaard is contrary to that which Kierkegaard himself gives later on, MacIntyre claims, with no supporting argument or evidence, that the internal evidence in *Either/Or* nevertheless supports his view. Expanding this claim, he further asserts that "a little later in *Philosophical Fragments* in 1845, Kierkegaard invokes this crucial new idea of radical and ultimate choice to explain how one becomes a Christian,"[13] an assertion that is anything but faithful to the book itself and totally ignores the problem of the book's pseudonymous authorship. MacIntyre believes this same thesis to be true also of *Fear and Trembling*, and claims that Kierkegaard speaks for himself in that book as well. In sum, the independent role of the pseudonyms is first acknowledged and then denied (an oft recurring pattern in Kierkegaard interpretation), and then "Kierkegaard" is adduced in support of a thesis he would never have recognized much less adopted.

Perhaps the best-known study of the pseudonymous authorship

is Mark C. Taylor's *Kierkegaard's Pseudonymous Authorship*. In his introductory chapter Taylor takes note of the "First and Last Declaration," which he acknowledges to be a complicating factor in the interpretation of the pseudonymous works. He regards these works as the most important writings for the understanding of Kierkegaard. "In the pseudonymous works *Kierkegaard* most carefully articulates *his ideas* and accomplishes his purpose of clarifying what it means to be an existing individual [emphasis mine]."[14] Taylor claims to discern, among the variety of points of view represented by the pseudonyms, a basic vision both of the nature of the self and of the attaining of authentic selfhood. He thus finds a coherence in Kierkegaard's total authorship, of which the pseudonymous works are regarded as the most important for its understanding. This means that Taylor is free to find Kierkegaard speaking through any of his poetic creations.

A striking example of this is found on p. 115. To support his contention that the self in Kierkegaard's view develops through free decision, Taylor quotes two passages, placing them next to each other—the first from *The Sickness unto Death*, the second from *Either/Or*, vol. 2:

> The self is composed of infinity and finiteness. But the synthesis is a relationship, and it is a relationship which, though it is derived, relates itself to itself, which means freedom. The self is freedom [Selvet er Frihed]. But freedom is the dialectical element in terms of possibility and necessity.[15]
>
> But what, then, is this self of mine: If I were required to define this, my first answer would be: It is the most abstract of all things, and yet at the same time it is the most concrete—It is freedom.

The *word* "freedom" is indeed common to both quotations, but its meaning in these two books is radically different. To choose oneself in one's eternal validity is a far cry from willing to be oneself through being grounded transparently in the Power that posits one.

Other examples can be adduced. Referring to the immediate aesthetic [in Either/Or] as pre-reflective, Taylor writes, "Kierkegaard comments on the stages of immediacy: 'Above all . . . one must avoid considering them as different degrees of consciousness, since even the last stage has not yet arrived at consciousness. I have always to do only with the immediate in its sheer immediacy.'"[16] This clearly is not Kierkegaard's comment; it is "A's."

Likewise, Judge William's pronouncements are taken as Kierkegaard's. A single example will suffice.

> Kierkegaard's discussion of the choice of oneself in one's eternal validity depends upon his conception of the concreteness of the self's existence.
>
> "He chooses himself, not in a finite sense . . . but in an absolute sense; and yet, in fact, he chooses himself and not another. This self which he then chooses is infinitely concrete, for it is in fact himself, and yet it is absolutely distinct from his former self, for he has chosen it absolutely."[17]

Here Judge William's well-worn theme of choosing oneself absolutely is ascribed to Kierkegaard—hardly to be reconciled with the notion in *The Sickness unto Death* of the self as posited by Another.

The views of other pseudonyms are also identified with Kierkegaard. In a footnote on p. 147 Taylor writes, "It should be noted that throughout *Fear and Trembling* Kierkegaard contrasts infinite resignation with faith. He argues that although infinite resignation is the last stage prior to faith, it is not faith itself. . . . What is involved in faith will become more evident in the next chapter." In that next chapter Taylor cites passages from such diverse sources as *Fragments* and *Training in Christianity*, but chiefly he appeals to the *Postscript*—that presumed repository of Christian doctrine!—in order to elucidate Kierkegaard's concept of faith.

One final illustration of Taylor's confusion. Concluding a discussion of sin, in which *The Sickness unto Death, The Concept of Dread, Training in Christianity*, and *Fear and Trembling* are randomly cited in support of his analysis, Taylor writes, "The recognition of the consequences of one's sin and the awareness of one's impotence to rectify the situation create in the individual a *need* for God and an *interest* in God's forgiving act in the incarnation."[18] "Interest" is an aesthetical category, suggesting preference, inclination; it is incompatable with Kierkegaard's Christian views. In a footnote he adds, "In a very interesting note in the *Postscript* . . . *Kierkegaard* comments on the relation between the need of the self and God: 'In this manner God certainly becomes a postulate'" [emphasis mine].[19] Taylor rightly notes the similarity between the argument presented here and Kant's notion of God as a postulate of the practical reason. What he fails to recognize is that there is a radical difference between Climacus' notion of God as a postulate—indeed, as a hypothesis in a thought experiment, presented with a large dose of irony, and Kierkegaard's understanding of the relation of the sinner to God that is to be found in *The Sickness unto Death*.

It is probably true that Kierkegaardian irony has by no means been overlooked by his interpreters, but oddly its full import has not been recognized. That Kierkegaard's master's thesis was on the concept of irony is known to all, as is the fact that there are many instances of irony in the corpus. What is not generally recognized is the ironic character of the pseudonymous authorship in form and purpose. Taylor's book is a nice illustration of what happens when the force and pervasiveness of the irony is not perceived and Kierkegaard's own account of what he was doing is quietly set aside or transformed into something quite different. The Index in Taylor's book has but three references to the word *irony*, all of which refer to *The Concept of Irony*. The first two are brief allusions to the book itself; in the last he suggests a parallel between the ironist and Johannes the Seducer, but he does not ascribe irony to "A's" writing as a whole nor to the Seducer's "Diary." Despite an initial recognition of Kierkegaard's claim that not a word of the pseudonyms is his, Taylor attributes their various doctrines to him in all seriousness, the irony ignored. Also ignored is Kierkegaard's own account of what he was doing.

In contrast, C. Stephen Evans writes with careful circumspection aboout the role of pseudonymity in Kierkegaard's authorship, with special reference to the writings of Johannes Climacus. In his book, *Kierkegaard's "Fragments" and "Postscript,"* Evans observes that "many writers have simply ignored the pseudonyms and cheerfully written long expositions of "Kierkegaard's" thought, gathered almost wholly from the pseudonymous works. Others have taken with great literalness Kierkegaard's assertion in the 'First and Last Declaration.' "[20] Evans opts for an intermediate position, arguing that while Kierkegaard intends that the pseudonyms should be regarded as independent beings with their own ideas, it does not follow that he did not share some of their ideas. Evans contends that, although there are decisive differences between Kierkegaard and his pseudonyms, some passages in the *Journals*, which are indisputably Kierkegaard's views, reflect exactly some that are found in the pseudonymous works. Climacus' notion of indirect communication is a case in point. Evans cites entries from the *Journals* in support of his interpretation.

As has been noted earlier, the pseudonymous works deal with concepts that are central to Christian thought, but they treat them in an aesthetical fashion. Love, despair, self, freedom (to mention a few) are *words* that are common to the pseudonymous works and to Kierkegaard's Christian writings, but these words have no common meaning. Evan's approach is open to difficulties because of this.

His analysis of the place of the pseudonyms in Kierkegaard's writing is carefully and fairly done. Missing, however, is a recognition of the role of irony in the pseudonymous authorship as a whole and consequently of the overall ironic purpose of *Fragments* and the *Postscript*. If the pervasive irony of the pseudonymous writings is overlooked, their structure is missed, and one can then only compare ideas and see which ones in the pseudonymous books bear a similarity to the same (?) ideas in the religious writings.

These reservations apart, Evans' book is one to be recommended.

One of Denmark's finest minds and a lifelong student of Kierkegaard, Johannes Sløk, professor at the University of Aarhus, has written extensively on Kierkegaard. Sløk takes seriously the independence of the pseudonyms and recognizes that the pseudonymous authorship presents a problem for the interpretation of Kierkegaard. Commenting on the difficulties which it poses, he writes in *Kierkegaards Univers*,

> It can be maintained that in a particular respect Kierkegaard is a profoundly unreliable author, and one can ask whether he ever wrote a book in which he unreservedly and without any ulterior motive personally meant every word.

Even the upbuilding writings—the so-called edifying discourses—which he published with S. Kierkegaard as author on the title page are in Sløk's opinion subject to doubt.

> It would not be unfair to assert that this "S. Kierkegaard" by a reverse twist is also a pseudonym. In any case one should not, as a matter of course, assume that it is genuine, that here one encounters the authentic Kierkegaard himself; and, when he calls one of the writings [*The Point of View*] "a straightforward report to history," one can be nearly certain that he is about to engage in a tampering with history.[21]

Sløk does not give reasons for this wide-ranging assertion. In correspondence with me he has written, "I am even inclined to view "Kierkegaard" (as the author of the upbuilding discourses) as a new pseudonym alongside of the others."[22] This kind of assertion has the force, ironically, of dissolving the problem into a chaos, for criteria are no longer possible for either asserting or denying anything about what Kierkegaard himself has said. Sløk's skepticism with regard to the possibility of finding "the real Kierkegaard" should serve, however, as a warning to those who would find Kierkegaard himself in every word he wrote.

Finally I would mention Josiah Thompson's essay in the volume entitled *Kierkegaard, A Collection of Critical Essays*, which he edited. This essay, "The Master of Irony," is an expansion of a chapter by the same title in his book, *Kierkegaard*. Thompson is totally faithful to Kierkegaard's own view of the pseudonymous authorship. He underscores the ghostly character of the pseudonyms, their lack of flesh and blood. "They are human but only abstractly so," but they are conscious of their abstractness. Their writings are characterized throughout by irony. "More than anything else it is this refusal of the pseudonym to be taken in by his dream, his steadfast irony, that gives these works their Kierkegaardian signature."[23] Thompson's essay underscores the fact that "the views of the pseudonyms are not Kierkegaard's. If anything, they are the views he has outlived or outthought."[24] In support of this Thompson quotes this journal entry: "As poet and thinker I have represented all things in the medium of imagination, myself living in resignation."[25]

Thompson concludes his essay with remarks from which I would offer these excerpts:

> If the pseudonymous works have shown us anything it is that *all the so-called "existential movements" end in failure.* . . .[26]
> This, I suspect, is precisely the aim of the pseudonyms, not to get the reader to make some impossible "existential movements," but to make the point that all such attempts at self-direction must fail. It is *failure*, I submit, the necessary failure of all human projects, that is at once the central meaning of the pseudonyms, as well as the source of their deepest religious import.[27]

While thus acknowledging that the pseudonymous works have

a religious import, Thompson does not develop the point, since it lies outside the scope of his topic.

As suggested earlier in the book, my own position is that the most powerful influence on Kierkegaard was Christianity. He understood his authorship to be a Christian vocation. While in substantial agreement with Thompson in respect to the pseudonymous writings and their ironic character, I have felt the need to go further and to relate Kierkegaard's undertaking in writing the pseudonymous works to his Christian concern. This in my judgment called for a consideration of two of his important Christian writings and a comparison of them with the pseudonymous production. It is to be regretted that the book containing Thompson's essay is no longer in print. He has written an outstanding essay on Kierkegaard—to my knowledge, the best.

NOTES

PREFACE

1. "A First and Last Declaration," included unpaged at the end of *Concluding Unscientific Postscript.*
2. See *The Point of View for my Work as an Author.*

CHAPTER ONE

1. *Either/Or*, p. 185. In an undated entry in his journal of 1843 he wrote, "Why do I not thrive like other children, why was I not swaddled in gladness, why did I come early to look into that kingdom of sighs, why was I born with a congenital anxiety which constantly let me look into it, why were nine months in my mother's womb enough to make me old, so that I was born not a child but an old man?" (IV B 141, p. 327)
2. I A 161.
3. X.2 A 3.
4. Josiah Thompson, *Kierkegaard*, p. 113.
5. X.1 A 281. The Danish word *dicter*, which is here translated as "poet," has no equivalent in English. A poet is one who gives aesthetic literary expression to an idea. Kierkegaard wrote no verse, but he is one of Denmark's great poets. His own use of the term reflects his firm conviction that there is a deep gulf between giving literary form to an idea and living it. See also Kierkegaard's description of the poet existence in *The Sickness unto Death*, pp. 77, 78.
6. X.5 A 146.
7. XI.1 A 340.
8. XII A 445.

9. Zealand is the large island on which Copenhagen is located.

10. Perhaps the best biography of Kierkegaard is by Josiah Thompson, *Kierkegaard.*

11. This does not include the pseudonym Anti-Climacus who, for reasons discussed in chapter 5, represents Kierkegaard's own view.

12. Until my wife and I discovered this during our visits in Denmark—and it took us some little time—we were constantly misunderstanding and being misunderstood because, like Horton the elephant, we meant what we said and said what we meant, and you don't do that in Denmark if you want to be understood. For example, when I was first teaching at a Danish folk-highschool, we said several times how much we were enjoying our stay. A few years later, when I was again teaching at the school, a colleague confided to me that he and some other colleagues had been quite concerned about our being unhappy at the school—precisely for our having said so many times the opposite! Had we contented ourselves with a laconic, "It's not so bad here," we would have made ourselves quite clear.

13. *The Concept of Irony*, p. 264f.

14. Ibid., p. 265.

15. *The Point of View for my Work as an Author*, pp. 39, 40.

16. Note here the double irony. There is a sense in which this is quite true. The one who is under an illusion is indeed a Christian in the common understanding of what a Christian is, and the writer is not a Christian in that sense.

17. *Point of View*, pp. 40, 41.

18. *Fear and Trembling*, p. 49.

19. Ibid., p. 74.

20. Ibid., p. 79. The word which is used here is *vidunder*, which means a marvel or prodigy. Kierkegaard reserves the word *mirakel* for his Christian writings.

21. X.6 B 79.

22. Lacking faith and misunderstanding its nature as well, Johannes is fundamentally frustrated: he is able to make the movement of infinite resignation, but "I cannot make the next movement, for the marvelous I cannot do—I can only be amazed at it." (p. 47).

23. At the beginning of the chapter entitled "Preliminary Expectoration," Johannes quotes what he calls an old adage: "Only the one who works gets bread," which is a misquotation of 2 Thessalonians 3:10, "He who will not work, shall not have food either."

24. Clearly Kierkegaard was also sending a message to Regine, that he had sacrificed marriage with her out of his love for her. This issue is discussed in chapter 6.

25. I will follow common usage and refer to the pseudonymous authors as the pseudonyms.

26. Josiah Thompson, *Kierkegaard*, ch. 12.

CHAPTER TWO

1. *Point of View*, p. 5.
2. Ibid., p. 22f.

3. Johannes Sløk, *Kierkegaards Univers*, Centrum Forlag, Denmark, p. 28.
4. *Point of View*, p. 35.
5. Ibid., p. 24.
6. It is an interesting coincidence that this insight bears a striking resemblance to a fundamental tenent of John Dewey's educational theory.
7. Those familiar with Kierkegaard may demur at what they regard as a glaring omission: the place which his broken relationship with Regine had in his writing. Kierkegaard acknowledged that the aim of the early pseudonymous works was to clarify what had happened between Regine and him — to reflect on the meaning of that painful episode in his life. Moreover, he wrote for her in the hope that she would read and understand. In this chapter, we are concerned with the more inclusive purpose of his writing, which was probably not fully articulated at the time, but which Kierkegaard came to regard as the central meaning of his life's work. The problem of the authorship's double motivation is discussed fully in chapter 6.
8. *Point of View*, p. 26.
9. Sløk, *Kierkegaards Univers*, p. 29.
10. *Either/Or*, 1:15.
11. Ibid., p. 30f.
12. Ibid., p. 235.
13. It is important to understand that the word *despair* does not refer to a feeling but to a condition or state of being. It is not a matter of feeling desperate but of living a life that contradicts one's true self.
14. *Either/Or*, 2:213.
15. Ibid., p. 214.
16. Ibid., 2:188.
17. Genesis 3:5.
18. *Either/Or*, 1:19–20.
19. *Ibid.*, 2:240.
20. Ibid., 1:320.
21. Ibid., 2:134.
22. Ibid., p. 137.
23. Ibid., p. 139.
24. *The Sickness unto Death*, p. 91.
25. "If a human existence is brought to the point where it lacks possibility, then it is in despair . . . What is decisive is that with God everything is possible." Ibid., p. 37, 38.
26. Ibid., p. 41.

CHAPTER THREE

1. The Danish title, *Filosofiske Smuler*, does not readily lend itself to translation; an alternative title might be "Bits of Philosophy," but none is really satisfactory.
2. *Philosophical Fragments*, p. 11.
3. Ibid., p. 12.
4. Having to do with midwifery.

5. Climacus uses the word *salighed,* blessedness, but *happiness* probably better expresses the Greek concept.

6. Ibid., p. 15.

7. Since the Moment, under this presupposition, is for the individual the source of his life's meaning and, consequently, of his authentic existence as an individual, the eternal comes into [his] existence only when he himself comes into relation with the Moment. Otherwise, he would not even be conscious of its being *the Moment,* even though he might have some disinterested or objective knowledge of that historical event.

8. *Fragments,* p. 16.

9. Ibid., p. 19.

10. Ibid., p. 198.

11. Ibid., p. 5.

12. Ibid., p. 34.

13. As pointed out in chapter 1, note 5, poet is a translation of the Danish *digter.* This is an untranslatable word, which does not mean one who writes verses but rather one who can give creative written form to thought and feeling. Kierkegaard is regarded as one of Denmark's greatest *digtere,* although he wrote no verse. In this context the poet is quite clearly one who is aesthetically interested in but not religiously concerned with what he is writing.

14. I have added the words in brackets to this sentence in order to make its meaning clear; in the original Danish the sentence is incomplete as it stands.

15. *Fragments,* p. 35.

16. "The Moment makes its appearance when an eternal resolve comes into relation with an incommensurable occasion." (p. 301). A relative historical event (all events in history are essentially relative to each other in their significance) bears, in this instance, an absolute meaning.

17. Note the choice of word, taken from the world of the theater.

18. *Fragments,* p. 137.

19. *Videnskab* is rooted in the word *viden* (knowledge) and has a broad range of meanings. Science is *naturvidenskab;* scholarship is *aandsvidenskab,* etc.

20. *Concluding Unscientific Postscript,* p. 18.

21. Ibid., p. 19 Cf. also the passage quoted on p. 28, footnote (17) supra.

22. As was indicated in chapter 2, p. 11, Kierkegaard had no high regard for Christendom. What commonly passed for "Christianity" was in his view a fundamental distortion of it.

23. Other similar passages can be cited, e.g., "Christianity has declared itself to be the eternal, essential truth which has come into being in time." (*Postscript,* p. 191).

24. Johannes does not hold fast to this error. Later in the book he quite correctly writes: "Christianity is not a doctrine but an existential communication. . . . If Christianity were a doctrine, it would *eo ipso* not be an opposite to speculative thought, but rather a phase within it." (p. 339).

25. Ibid., p. 330.

26. Ibid., p. 330.

27. Ibid., p. 19.

28. Ibid., p. 20. Once again, it should be noted that the problem is the relationship of the individual to Christianity, not to God in Christ.

29. Ibid., p. 23.
30. Ibid., p. 116. Christianity, as the source of one's salvation, *exists* as such only for one for whom it is saving truth; otherwise it is an historical phenomenon of general significance, which one views objectively with more or less interest.
31. Ibid., p. 118.
32. Ibid., p. 146.
33. Ibid., p. 171, 173, 175.
34. Ibid., p. 164 ff.
35. Ibid., p. 174.
36. Ibid., p. 178. "Fantastic" indicates that it is a product of fantasy.
37. Ibid., p. 178.
38. Ibid., p. 182.
39. Ibid., p. 182.
40. Ibid., p. 178.
41. See the discussion of Anselm and Climacus on p. 3 supra.
42. *Postscript*, p. 547.

CHAPTER FOUR

1. *Either/Or*, i:15.
2. *Works of Love*, p. 20.
3. Ibid., p. 26.
4. Ibid., p. 25.
5. Ibid., p. 27.
6. Kierkegaard calls his book, *Kjerlighedens Gerninger*, love's works; this, in contradistinction to *kjerlighedsgerninger*, which means works of charity or good works. As is so often the case, the original makes the distinction more neatly than can be done in translation.
7. *Works of Love*, p. 30. Again, it is impossible neatly to make the distinction in translation between *kjerlighedsgerninger* and *kjerlighedens gerninger*—works of love (good works) and love's works.
8. Ibid., p. 35. Similarly, the psychiatrist, Eric Fromm, has observed that the selfish man does not love himself too much but too little. If a person does not love himself, if he nourishes, perhaps unconsciously, a deep dislike of himself, he cannot love another, because he cannot believe that he himself is lovable and that another person would be able to love him. Therefore, he feels that he has to grasp after the recognition and acceptance that he believes would never freely be given him. He demands for himself anything (or anyone) that he can lay claim to or coerce, without having any sense of responsibility for them. He is preoccupied with his own need. In contrast, there is a kind of self-love which is not selfish but, on the contrary, expresses our humanity, and it is this love of self that Fromm recognized to be the necessary condition of neighbor love. In Kierkegaard's view this love of the heart presupposes the firm conviction that the self is essentially—to use St. Paul's words—rooted and grounded in love, in God's love, which is the hidden source of every authentic life.
9. Ibid., p. 39.

10. Danish has the two words *kjerlighed* and *forkjerlighed,* love and (as Lowrie and the Hongs have translated it) preferential love. Kierkegaard also speaks of spontaneous love and erotic love—all of these to be differentiated from love in the sense of neighbor love. English has scant resources for distinguishing between the various affects and relationships that are, preforce, included in the one word, love.

11. *Works of Love,* p. 36.

12. Ibid., p. 38f. Kierkegaard's assertion that finding a friend can be a long, hard job may sound strange to American ears but not to Danish, especially in Kierkegaard's time. Danes tend to have only two or three [close] friends [*venner*] in their lives; the others, whom we would call friends, are acquaintances [*bekendte*].

13. Ibid., p. 65. The Danish word for neighbor is *naesten,* literally the one next to you.

14. I think here, primarily, of the Greek, and I do not use the word pejoratively.

15. It is this aspect of love that is absolutized in Volume 1 of *Either/Or.*

16. *Works of Love,* p. 65.

17. This paragraph is a paraphrase. Ibid., p. 70. Neighbor love does not exclude preferential love; it robs it of its imperialism—its sin. The influence of Augustine's thought is clearly evident here. In referring to the next human being, Kierkegaard is making a play on the word for neighbor, *naesten*— the one next to you.

18. Ibid., p. 73.

19. Ibid., p. 74.

20. Ibid., p. 49.

21. Ibid., p. 54.

22. Ibid., pp. 159, 161.

23. Ibid., p. 344. See footnote (8), chapter 1, in which the opposite is said.

24. *Either/Or,* 1:255.

25. Ibid., p. 268.

26. Ibid., p. 277.

27. Ibid., p. 299.

28. Johannes does claim that he is doing something for Cordelia: that he is bringing out her femininity; but her life as a person is of no concern to him.

29. *Either/Or,* 1:305.

30. Ibid., p. 371.

31. Constantin Constantius, another of Kierkegaard's aesthetical pseudonyms, was later to deal with the general problem of repetition in a little book by that name.

32. Ibid., 2:22.

33. Ibid., p. 26.

34. Ibid., p. 48.

35. Ibid., p. 49.

36. Ibid., Vol. 1, pp. 243, 244.

37. Ibid., 2:26. Anyone acquainted with Anti-Climacus' analysis of despair in *The Sickness unto Death,* which expresses Kierkegaard's deepest Christian convictions, will blanche at the self-righteous purity of soul claimed here.

Anti-Climacus' confession that, with God, all things are possible is here a claim made for the religious individual.

38. Revelation is here not a theological category; it means the revealing of one's motives and purposes.
39. Either/Or, 2:98.
40. Ibid., p. 100.

CHAPTER FIVE

1. *Either/Or*, 2:134.
2. Ibid., p. 143.
3. Ibid., p. 143.
4. Ibid., p. 149.
5. Ibid., p. 150.
6. Ibid., p. 162.
7. Ibid., p. 162. The judge's parenthetical remark is typical of his studied determination to ascribe to "A" some vestige of the ethical. Were "A" a human being rather than an abstraction, this would not be incorrect. It must be remembered, however, that Kierkegaard's aesthetes are types, not persons.
8. Ibid., pp. 174, 175.
9. In the foregoing paragraphs, as well as in subsequent passages, the word *despair* occurs frequently. Again, it is important to remember that despair does *not* refer to a feeling. Johannes, the seducer, to take one example, would strenuously deny that he was in despair—or felt himself to be in despair. On the contrary, he was experiencing the most exquisite pleasure. Under some circumstances, despair may manifest itself as melancholy, but that is by no means its most frequent expression. Its most common form is to be unconscious that one is in despair. Kierkegaard deals with despair at length in *The Sickness unto Death*. Suffice it to say here that despair refers to a life whose self-affirmation is in reality self-negation. The despairing person is destroying his life in living it. The judge's understanding of despair is, of course, less radical than that presented in *Sickness*.
10. Ibid., p. 177.
11. See p. 39f. supra.
12. *Either/Or*, Vol. 2, p. 179. One is tempted to agree that the judge is no logician.
13. Ibid., p. 179.
14. See p. 39f. supra.
15. X.1 A 517.
16. Kierkegaard intended to publish *The Sickness unto Death*, along with some other religious works, under his own name (cf. Pap X.2, A 147), but for a number of reasons he was reluctant to do so, and he hit upon the idea of another pseudonym. "This pseudonym was adopted merely to relieve his own fine feeling of propriety. It must be understood also that this form of pseudonymity was totally different from that which hitherto he had used . . ., for these later works were the sincerest expression of his own belief, and he had expected to publish them under his own name." (Lowrie, Introduction to *The Sickness unto Death*, p. 138). For a full discussion of the

reasons for adopting the pseudonym, Anti-Climacus, see Hong, Introduction to *The Sickness unto Death.*

17. Sickness unto Death, p. 13. Subsequent unfootnoted quotations are from pp. 13 and 14.
18. I shall follow the translator in using the term 'man' in its generic meaning. Anti-Climacus uses the word *menneske,* which is the Danish word for generic man, or human being, as it is often translated. But sometimes human being is awkward, and I have decided in favor of man, although I am cognizant of what some regard as the sexist connotations of the generic form. Incidentally, in gender *menneske* is neuter, thus saving the Danes, in this regard, at least from sexist arguments.
19. The text has "freedom and necessity," but the use of freedom here appears to be a mistake. On p. 29, Anti-Climacus writes, "The self is freedom. But freedom is the dialectical element in the terms possibility and necessity." Every subsequent mention of freedom conforms to this statement, whereas the self as a synthesis of freedom and necessity is incompatible with Anti Climacus' main thesis. Kierkegaard did little or no editing of his books; he wrote them and sent them off to the publisher pretty much unrevised. This error appears to have escaped his notice. See *Kierkegaard's Pseudonymous Authorship,* p. 88 note, where Kierkegaard's slip is noted.
20. The use of the first person singular is virtually a requirement here. In his religious works, Kierkegaard was writing to "his reader"—to the individual who could truly hear him. Moreover, when one thinks about the self, one is soon compelled to realize that one can never experience what it is to be *a* self but can only reflect on the mystery of being *myself.*
21. *Either/Or,* 2:150. See p. 121 supra, note 5.
22. Because he *wills despairingly* to be a self that he is not, he cannot escape from his despair precisely because he *wills* not to.
23. *Sickness unto Death,* p. 61. While Lowrie's translation of this last sentence is not literally accurate, it captures beautifully the thrust of Kierkegaard's confession.
24. Ibid., p. 77. *Forestilling,* which is here translated as conception, is not to be confused with concept. It means literally something that is placed before, and is perhaps better rendered by "notion" or "image."
25. Ibid., p. 82.
26. Ibid., p. 83.
27. The ethical position of Judge William is derived from Kant; and the role of God in his thought is likewise tinged with the Kantian position. God is ancillary to the ethical life, a practical postulate of moral autonomy.

CHAPTER SIX

1. *Phantasi.* See Kierkegaard's comments on the despair of the fantastical in *Sickness unto Death,* p. 30f.
2. *Sickness unto Death,* p. 77. Speaking of a poet-existence in the direction of the religious, he writes on the same page, "He loves God above all, God who is his only consolation in his secret anguish, and yet he loves the an-

guish and will not give it up. He would like so very much to be himself before God, but with the exclusion of the fixed point where the self suffers; there in despair he does not will to be himself."

3. The title which the pseudonymous editor of "A's" papers, Victor Eremita, gives to a number of short, lyrical, aphoristic reflections, which, supposedly, he found on bits of loose paper in an old secretary; they stand at the beginning of vol. 1.
4. IV A 216, p. 86.
5. *Either/Or*, 1:15.
6. *Opbygge* means literally to build up. It has usually been translated as edifies, e.g., *Edifying Discourses*.
7. IV A 107.
8. This is found in *Stages on Life's Way*, Studies by Sundry Persons, collected, forwarded to the press and published by Hilarius Bookbinder. It is a long, drawn out and only slightly disguised rehashing of the broken engagement.
9. IV A 107.
10. *Point of View*, p. 163.
11. X.1 A 266. The final sentence, a difficult one in the Danish, is here the Hongs' translation. Danish has two words for Providence. *Forsynet* has more the connotation of providing, whereas *Styrelsen*, which Kierkegaard uses, points to the divine guidance, or governance.
12. X.1 A 266.
13. *Point of View*, pp. 72, 73.
14. The Danish word, *opdrage*, means both to educate and to bring up.
15. *Point of View*, pp. 73, 74.
16. Ibid., p. 22.
17. Ibid., p. 23.
18. Ibid., p. 24.
19. Ibid., p. 25.
20. Ibid., p. 29.
21. Ibid., p. 38.

APPENDIX

1. See Thompson, "The Master of Irony."
2. See John W. Elrod, *Being and Existence in Kierkegaard's Pseudonymous Works* (Princeton: Princeton University Press).
3. Louis Poyman, *The Logic of Subjectivity* (University: University of Alabama Press, 1984), p. x.
4. Ibid., p. 47.
5. S. Kierkegaard, *Philosophical Fragments*, p. 32f. See also p. 63f., supra.
6. Thulstrup quietly shifts from "the god" [guden] to "God" [gud], presumably to make his theological points.
7. *Philosophical Fragments*, p. lxxiii f.
8. See p. 64, supra.
9. MacIntyre, Alasdair, *After Virtue*, University of Notre Dame Press, 1981, pp. 40, 41.

10. Ibid.
11. MacIntyre makes an essentially Sartrian interpretation of Kierkegaard (Judge William).
12. MacIntyre, p. 41.
13. Ibid., p. 41.
14. Taylor, *Kierkegaard's Pseudonymous Writings*, p. 19.
15. Taylor's translation of the last sentence is inaccurate. It should read, "But freedom is the dialectical [element] in the determinants possibility and necessity."
16. Taylor, p. 139.
17. Ibid., p. 187.
18. Ibid., p. 289 f.
19. Ibid., p. 290.
20. Evans, *Kierkegaard's "Fragments" and "Postscript,"* p. 7.
21. Sløk, Johannes, *Kierkegaards Univers*, Centrum, København, 1983, p. 8.
22. In the same letter Sløk also writes, "For my part it has always been a fundamental matter, that Kierkegaard's authorship was a continuing and exhaustive discussion of the problem which 'A' represents, but a discussion that nowhere reaches its conclusion—nor can it reach its conclusion." Note that it is the problem which 'A' represents, not a problem he presents, for of course 'A' presents none, because he recognizes none. For Sløk this constitutes a problem, one that is not a philosophic problem but an existential one, and is solved (or dissolved) only by the way in which the individual lives his life.
23. See Thompson, *Kierkegaard, A Collection of Critical Essays*, p. 111.
24. Ibid., p. 112.
25. Ibid., p. 113, VIII.1 A 650.
26. Ibid., p. 137 f.
27. Ibid., p. 160 f.

BIBLIOGRAPHY

PRIMARY SOURCES

In Danish

Søren Kierkegaard, Samlede Vaerker, udgivet af A. B. Drachmann, J. L. Heiberg, og H. O. Lange. København: Gyldendal, 1962.
Søren Kierkegaards Papirer ved Niels Thulstrup. København: Gyldendal, 1986.

English Translations (Relevant to the problem of pseudonymity)

Concluding Unscientific Postscript. Trans. by David F. Swenson and Walter Lowrie. Princeton: Princeton University Press, 1941.
Edifying Discourses. 4 vols. Trans. by David F. and Lillian Marvin Swenson. Minneapoilis: Augsburg Publishing House, 1943ff.
Edifying Discourses: A Selection. Trans. by David F. and Lillian Marvin Swenson. New York: Harper Torchbooks, 1958.
Either/Or. Vol. 1 trans. by David F. and Lillian Marvin Swenson: vol. 2 trans. by Walter Lowrie. Princeton: Princeton University Press, 1971.
Fear and Trembling/Repetition. Ed. and trans. by Howard V. Hong and Edna H. Hong. Princeton: Princeton University Press, 1983.
Journals and Papers. Ed. and trans. by Howard V. and Edna H. Hong. Bloomington: Indiana University Press, 1967ff.
Philosophical Fragments. Trans. by David F. Swenson, trans. rev. by Howard V. Hong, Introduction and Commentary by Niels Thulstrup. Princeton: Princeton University Press, 1962.
Stages on Life's Way. Trans. by Walter Lowrie. New York: Shocken Books, 1967.
The Concept of Anxiety. Ed. and trans. by Reidar Thomte. Princeton: Princeton University Press, 1980.

105

The Concept of Irony. Trans. by Lee M. Capel. Bloomington: Indiana University Press, 1968.

The Point of View of My Work as an Author: A Report to History. Trans. by Walter Lowrie. New York: Harper Torchbook, 1962.

The Sickness unto Death. Ed. and trans. by Howard V. Hong and Edna H. Hong. Princeton: Princeton University Press, 1980.

Training in Christianity. Trans. by Walter Lowrie. Princeton: Princeton University Press, 1971.

Works of Love. Trans. by Howard and Edna Hong. New York: Harper Torchbook, 1962.

Lindhardt, P. G. "Subjektiviteten er sandheden." *Kierkegaardiana*, vol. 5. Kobenhavn: Munksgaard, 1964.

Malantschuk, Gregor. *Kierkegaard's Thought.* Princeton: Princeton University Press, 1971.

Malantschuk, Gregor. *Indforelse i Søren Kierkegaards Forfatterskab.* Kobenhavn: Munksgaard, 1952.

Perkins, Robert L., ed. *Kierkegaard's Fear and Trembling: Critical Appraisals,* University: University of Alabama Press, 1981.

Rhode, Peter P. *Søren Kierkegaard.* København: Thaning & Appel, 1960.

Sløk, Johannes. *Kierkegaard.* København: Gad Forlag, 1961.

Sløk, Johannes. *Kierkegaards Univers.* København: Centrum, 1983.

Swenson, David F. *Something About Kierkegaard.* Minneapolis: Augsburg, 1945.

Taylor, Mark C. *Kierkegaard's Pseudonymous Authorship.* Princeton: Princeton University Press, 1973.

Thompson, Josiah. *Kierkegaard.* New York: Knopf, 1973.

Thompson, Josiah. "The Master of Irony." essay in Josiah Thompson, *Kierkegaard: A Collection of Critical Essays.* pp. 103–163. New York: Doubleday, 1972.

Thomte, Reidar. *Kierkegaard's Philosophy of Religion.* Princeton: Princeton University Press, 1948.

SECONDARY SOURCES

Brandt, Frithiof. *Søren Kierkegaard.* Copenhagen: Det Danske Selskab, 1963.

Colette, Jacques, O. P. *Kierkegaard: The Difficulty of being a Christian.* Notre Dame, Ind: University of Notre Dame Press, 1969.

Crites, Stephen. "Pseudonymous Authorship as Art and as Act." In Josiah Thompson, ed., *Kierkegaard: A Collection of Critical Essays,* pp. 183–229. New York: Doubleday, 1972.

Crites, Stephen. *In the Twilight of Christendom.* Chambersburg, Pa.: American Academy of Religion, 1971.

Evans, C. Stephen. *Kierkegaard's "Fragments" and "Postscript."* Atlantic Highlands, N.J.: Humanities Press, 1983.

Geismar, Eduard. *Lectures on the Religious Thought of Søren Kierkegaard.* Minneapolis: Augsburg, 1937.

Gill, Jerry H. *Essays on Kierkegaard.* Minneapolis: Burgess, 1969.

Hansen, Knud. *Søren Kierkegaard*. København: Gyldendal, 1954.
Hohlenberg, Johannes. *Den Ensommes Vej*. København: Aschehoug Dansk Forlag, 1968.
Hohlenberg, Johannes. *Søren Kierkegaard*. København: Aschehough Dansk Forlag, 1963.

INDEX

DATE DUE

APR 15 1992			